ADVANCE PRAISE

"I've been a sales professional for thirty years, and I've read countless books on the subject, but rarely have I encountered a book that combines both heartfelt personal stories and real-world industry research as effectively as *The Sales Tightrope*. I read it in one sitting Sunday afternoon. An extremely fun and informative read. It's a home run!"

— **Dave Chiasson**
Sales Specialist

"Katie dives right in with a wealth of practical real-world research that is backed up by the field experience of someone who wins time after time after time. If you or the people you manage have the work ethic to succeed, the advice Katie gives you from the first page on will translate into exponentially more success. I have had the privilege of working directly with Katie as well as hiring her to teach my teams on multiple occasions. I can personally vouch for the fact that she is the real deal and the truths contained in this book aren't an academic exercise, they are real-world practices you can use to be more successful today."

— **Robert Wittwer**
Senior VP Professional Services and Operations | Ascom Americas

"Katie Mullen's *The Sales Tightrope* provides excellent sales guidance for both rookies and seasoned veterans. It seamlessly combines real-life selling scenarios with extensive customer research to illustrate suggested salesperson behaviors & possible customer responses. As a former sales manager, I highly recommend this book for both you and your team members. It offers outstanding 'how to' insight for your rookies and notable 'refresher tips' for your veterans. A nice bonus to hand out at your next sales meeting!"

— **Bob Mesalam**
Retired Sales Executive

"Five years ago, Katie Mullen was referred to me by a VP of Marketing who had worked closely with her at a major medical device company. I was looking for someone to work with our sales team on improving their selling skills. Katie listened to me, was friendly, seemed to understand my concerns, and had a genuine interest in my needs. After a brief conversation with her, I knew she was the right person for our team. Year after year the sales team asked Katie to come back to deliver more training. They loved her training!

Katie's new book, *The Sales Tightrope* delivers such a simple message–sales is not rocket science, there is an art to it–and it all comes down to being interested in the customer. Ask the customer what they think. Be friendly. The book focuses on simple direct ways to be successful by communicating with customers in short, succinct language. The Wedge Questioning process Katie discusses in her book helped our sales team shorten the sales cycle by getting to the customers' pain points quickly to move the sales forward.

We have practiced the sales process Katie has written about in her new book for the past five years with great sales success. I would highly recommend reading this insightful and enlightening sales book if you want to improve your selling experience and results."

— **Pamela Jerdee**

Senior Training & Education Manager | Fresenius Medical Care North America

"Have you ever wondered why your sales approach is not creating the results you had hoped? Have you ever been confused about exactly which activities create the most impact or what to include in your big presentation? What should you do when the sales call is going badly or when a prospect stops calling you back? Is social media really worth the time investment?

The Sales Tightrope by Katie Mullin answers these questions and much more. It is a no-nonsense, actionable guide to approaching, engaging, and serving your clients. Katie's research shows us what leads to trust and credibility—straight from customers' mouths.

The Sales Tightrope is a must-read for sales reps and sales managers who want to impact the world by providing their products and services in a consistent, repeatable way."

— **Michael Barrovecchio**

President | CAPO Leadership Consulting

THE SALES TIGHTROPE

A RESEARCH-BASED GUIDE TO NOT ANNOYING CUSTOMERS AND STILL BEING A TOP PERFORMER

KATIE MULLEN

The Sales Tightrope © 2023 by Katie Mullen

Published by Streamline Books
www.streamlinebookspublishing.com

All rights reserved.

No part of this book may be reproduced, distributed, or transmitted in any form or by any means, including photocopying, recording, or other electronic or mechanical methods, without the written permission from the author, except in the case of brief quotations embodied in a book review.

Cover design by Hannah Crabb and Renee Schultz

ISBN:
979-8-89165-036-7 (paperback)
979-8-89165-037-4 (hardback)
979-8-89165-038-1 (e-book)

September 14, 2023

Disclaimer: Although the publisher and the author have made every effort to ensure that the information in this book was correct at press time and while this publication is designed to provide accurate information in regard to the subject matter covered, the publisher and the author assume no responsibility for errors, inaccuracies, omissions, or any other inconsistencies herein and hereby disclaim any liability to any party for any loss, damage, or disruption caused by errors or omissions, whether such errors or omissions result from negligence, accident, or any other cause.

This is for my family. Thanks for always supporting me and believing in me.

CONTENTS

THE SALES TIGHTROPE

Introduction   3

SECTION I
THE CARDINAL RULE IN SALES: UNDERSTAND YOUR CUSTOMER

1. CUSTOMER INSIGHTS: RESEARCH FROM REAL CUSTOMERS   9
   The Results   11
   Chapter Summary   22

2. STOP ANNOYING CUSTOMERS: UNDERSTAND THEIR PERSONALITY PROFILE   25
   Methods to Identify Different Personality Styles   30
   Gaining Their Trust   32
   How Can You Make Small Talk if You're a Driver or Analytic?   33
   Put It into Practice   34
   Chapter Summary   36

SECTION II
PROSPECTING FOR NEW BUSINESS: A WINNING FORMULA

3. THE SCIENCE BEHIND WRITING A KILLER EMAIL   41
   How to Make Your Emails More Effective   42
   5 Elements of a Killer Prospect Letter   44
   Crafting a Good Subject Line   48
   Common Grammar Mistakes to Avoid   50
   What to Do When They Don't Reply   51
   Timing It Right: When Should You Email?   53
   Chapter Summary   54

4. THE ART OF FINDING CUSTOMERS ... 57
   - Leads Go Cold Quickly ... 59
   - Finding the Right Person ... 60
   - The Gatekeeper ... 61
   - The C-Suite Gatekeeper ... 63
   - How to Strategize and Prioritize Your Accounts ... 64
   - Chapter Summary ... 66

5. TACKLING THE FIRST 10 SECONDS OF THE PROSPECTING CALL ... 69
   - Keep It Casual ... 73
   - Be Friendly ... 75
   - Timing and Cadence ... 75
   - Talk Tracks/Scripts ... 79
   - Voicemail Strategy ... 79
   - The Best-Kept Secret to Prospecting ... 80
   - Chapter Summary ... 82

6. UNCOVERING PAIN POINTS USING THE MAGIC WEDGE QUESTION ... 85
   - Secrets Revealed ... 87
   - Pre-Call Data Gathering ... 89
   - Disarming Them ... 91
   - The Wedge Question Explained ... 93
   - Creating *Your* Wedge Questions ... 95
   - Qualifying Questions ... 99
   - When You Hear "We're Just Not Interested" ... 103
   - Chapter Summary ... 104

7. THE SECRET TO GREAT MEETINGS AND PRESENTATIONS ... 107
   - How to Focus on Them: Presentations ... 109
   - Consider Starting With a Story as Your "Hook" ... 111
   - What's Next ... 114
   - How to Focus on Them: Meetings ... 116
   - Virtual Presentations Done Right ... 120
   - Preparation Is Key ... 121
   - The Technology ... 121
   - Chapter Summary ... 124

SECTION III
NEW WAYS TO SELL: TOOLS YOU MIGHT NOT THINK YOU NEED

8. SOCIAL SELLING: WHY LINKEDIN IS YOUR NEXT
   BEST FRIEND 129
   Appealing to the Right Audience 131
   6 Key Aspects for a Strong *Customer-Facing* Profile 132
   Posting Value 139
   Chapter Summary 144

9. VIDEO MESSAGING: THE SECRET WEAPON OF
   SALES 147
   Chapter Summary 154

   Conclusion: Bringing It All Together 157

   QR Code: Digital Downloads 160
   Appendix A: Mirroring Personality Styles Worksheet ... 161
   Appendix B: Letter Worksheet 163
   Appendix C: Call Script Worksheet 165
   Appendix D: Product Features and Wedge Questions Worksheet 167
   Appendix E: LinkedIn Self-Evaluation Worksheet 169
   Acknowledgments 171
   About the Author 173
   Notes 175

THE SALES TIGHTROPE

INTRODUCTION

After thirteen years of a successful sales career, I found myself in quite a pickle. My husband was finishing his residency in orthopedic surgery, and we found out he had to move to Denver for a sports medicine fellowship with the Denver Broncos. It was all very exciting, except for one problem: how would I run my territory of Kansas, Missouri, and Nebraska from *Denver*?

I spent several weeks trying to figure this out. With two young kids, it would be tricky because of the overnight travel, but maybe I could make it work. Perhaps I could bring them with me when I traveled, and they could stay with my parents, or maybe my husband could watch them when he wasn't working. But, reality settled in, and I realized driving two kids on an eight-hour commute was impractical. And my husband's job with the Broncos wouldn't allow him to go in late to help drop the kids off.

I finally admitted it: it wasn't going to work. It was time to hand over my carefully-curated territory, but I *really* didn't want to. When I first started with my company, our products were brand-new. I had zero percent market share, so it was a rough first year, but I did it. I hustled, built a loyal customer base, and made good money. But, that was all over now. With great sadness, I helped hire the new rep, gave him some tips and pointers, and packed up my minivan to head west.

I have to admit, we did have an amazing year in Denver. My kids were young, and we taught them to ski and camp and live the good life. I got a few consulting jobs, and we made it work financially. After our year was up, it was time to move back to Kansas, and I was itching to get back into sales. Right after we got back, I met another mom, who was the CEO and owner of a successful speaker's bureau, and she asked me to join her start-up sales team. I got along well with her, and she was also an incredibly inspiring business person. Even though it was different from what I'd been doing, it seemed like a fun challenge, and I agreed to try it.

Several of us started at the same time. We could call on anyone who wasn't already a customer. Our job was strictly to find new clients, and we had a huge volume of potential customers, so I was excited to get started.

During our first sales meeting, the owner of the company asked me if I would teach the team some of my techniques I had used during my days of selling medical equipment. She knew I had also done extensive customer research for my consulting role during my year in Denver. I *did* have a wealth of knowledge to share, so I agreed, but when I opened my mouth to start explaining some of my techniques, one of the new reps interrupted and said, "I mean, it's not rocket science, is it?"

Everyone laughed, and the moment passed. Someone changed the subject, and we all went our separate ways to our own houses and began the process of picking up the phone to find new clients.

Nine months later, I was having great success. I had landed several large customers, and the rest of the team was struggling. The owner of the company came to me and said, "Katie, we need to

Introduction

know what you're doing. You've found so many good clients and you're the only one having any success."

I thought back to that first day. The truth is, sales is *not* rocket science, but there *is* an art to it, and it all comes down to being interested in the customer. What are their daily frustrations? What does their staff complain about?

Only when you begin to understand your customers can you learn the art of sales, so that you, too, can land big clients. This is not a book of sales theory. This book contains practical advice—advice that works and has been proven through research.

Whether you're brand-new to sales or looking for a refresher on research-based techniques to succeed, the advice, data, and strategies in this book are proven to work. If you follow where the research leads, your customers will love you and you'll never be out of work. So, let's get to it.

SECTION I

THE CARDINAL RULE IN SALES: UNDERSTAND YOUR CUSTOMER

1

CUSTOMER INSIGHTS: RESEARCH FROM REAL CUSTOMERS

Several years ago, I saw a Facebook post that made me stop and think. It was from a child psychologist who asked her young patients what they really thought of their parents, and what they wished their parents knew about them. Here are some of the answers from the children who were surveyed:

- "Being alone in my room is OK… it doesn't mean that I'm suicidal or sad." (sixteen-year-old)
- "Taking away all that I love doesn't motivate me. It leaves me feeling hopeless." (ten-year-old)
- "My dog gets more attention than I do. Dad said it is because the dog can't talk, so I stopped talking." (seven-year-old)
- "My mom says 'in a minute' and hours go by. This is why I yell and demand. She forgets me." (sixteen-year-old)[1]

Parents generally have good intentions. And yet, sometimes the decisions we make on how to discipline, what we say, and how we interact with our children don't land the way we wanted. The problem is that so often we don't realize it, because we generally don't take the time to ask *children* for their feedback.

If parenting experts spent more time asking kids about their perspectives, as the "client" in a parenting relationship, I predict we would know a lot more about parenting as a society. There are so many books about parenting out there, written by adults, for adults, and a big gaping hole for books written with a child's point of view.

I think the same can be said about sales books. There are so many books out there written by "experts" on how to sell. Many of them are excellent, and will be referenced throughout this book.

Yet, in all my years of reading books and researching selling techniques, I've never come across anyone who asked the *customers* what they think. That's where I think experts have fallen short.

Who better to comment on the performance and process of vendors than the customers themselves? I had a sense this would be incredibly powerful, so I searched and searched for a book to read. I scoured the Internet for data. I looked for podcasts, but I kept coming up short. It didn't seem like anyone had ever asked customers for their feedback on people trying to sell them stuff.

For years, I kept an eye out for a book on this topic, and never came across one. When I started my own business, I decided to remedy this. I began a long process of interviewing hundreds of customers from all over the country. I asked a standard set of questions, such as:

- What are your pet peeves when you receive a cold call?
- What general advice would you give salespeople?
- Do you call vendors back when they leave a voicemail?
- What is your advice for formal presentations?

The answers were often surprising, and a common theme presented itself: what customers want are genuine, honest sales reps, who are interested in *them*, and not trying to *be* interesting. In the end, it's all human nature. People care about themselves. *Customers, especially, care about themselves, not you.*

The Results

Below you will find a summary of the trends from my research. It will help you understand how customers think, so you can ask questions that will provide you the answers you need: answers that will help you get the meeting, then the presentation, then the deal, and eventually, a long-term customer.

Cold Call Pet Peeves

The first question I asked during my customer interviews was: "What are your pet peeves when a vendor calls you out of the blue for the first time (a true 'cold call')?" Here are the top five most common responses:

1. **Negative selling.** Many vendors think they are being authentic and that it will win them points with the customer if they're honest about the competition. Unfortunately, this is a myth. Customers hate it when you bash the competitor (even if the information you're sharing is true). They will start to feel like they need to defend the competitor, which is the last thing you want. Instead, ask questions about what the customers need, so it plants a seed in their head. Then, they will ask the competitor if they are capable of providing that special feature.

For example, let's say you're selling fetal monitors for babies, and you know you're the only ones on the market who can monitor triplets. You happen to know that the hospital you're visiting is a Level III birthing center, meaning they deliver specialty care and handle complicated deliveries. So, maybe you ask the question, "Would it ever be important to you to have a device that could monitor triplets?" They respond that it's not common, but it does happen. You explore this with them, and ask more questions about their process. You know that your competitors won't be able to do this, so when the customer asks your competitor the question, they'll find the gaping hole in their capabilities. Bam. Now they realize the limitations of the competitor, but you didn't have to tell them. Instead of bashing the competitor, you led the customer down the path, so they could find out for themselves, and they still got the information. It's much more powerful this way.

2. Keeping them on the phone. Just hang up on them. Truly. If they say they're walking into a meeting, apologize and hang up. Don't keep them for another thirty seconds while you explain who you are, why you're calling, and ask for a better time to call. Just hang up, and then when you call back or email, you can remind them that you let them off the phone by saying something like, "I'm sorry I caught you at a bad time yesterday. Is this better?" I can't tell you how many times I've been thanked for doing this. It starts to build trust and will set you apart from all the other sales reps who don't do this. When they say they're busy, believe them.

3. Name-dropping. I know what you're thinking. You might *actually* know someone within the facility, so what should you do? Just don't lead with it. Introduce yourself, plain and simple, and then silence is your best friend. Let the customer start leading the conversation, and then you can eventually mention that Jane Smith recommended you call.

4. Being pushy. This one might seem obvious. It's a sales rep's biggest fear. *Do I come off as pushy? Like a used car salesman?* The truth is, many of us might *seem* pushy, but we're not trying to be. It's often just a symptom of our nerves. We're probably talking too fast or not allowing any silence. Awkward silence is your friend, and will make you seem less pushy.

5. Saying, "I can save you money." Many customers shared that they really don't like it when someone opens a cold call promising to save them money. This surprised me. As sales reps, we are often taught to demonstrate the ROI to catch the customer's attention. So, why are customers saying it's a pet peeve? For several reasons. First, everyone says it, so it's become like white noise: Just something people say, not something that is real. Second, you have no idea how much the customer is currently spending, so how would you know how much they can save? Lastly, the person you're talking to likely did the negotiating on the current deal, so if you say you can save them money, you're kind of telling them they did a bad job. You can still cover this eventually to help you win the deal, but never lead with it.

Will Customers Call You Back?

It probably comes as no surprise that when asked, only 8% of customers said they would call back a cold caller. And honestly, that's the number that *said* they would call back. The actual number is probably even smaller. That's not to say there isn't a time and place to leave a message for a customer, but just realize that it must also come with an email or another phone call. Each time they hear your voice or see your name, that trust is continuing to build, slowly but surely. This only applies if you're polite and not pushy.

What Is the Top Advice Customers Give to Sales Reps?

When conducting my research, I asked the question, "Let's pretend your niece or nephew is going into sales and asks for your advice. What would you say?" Of course, I got a wide variety of answers on this, since it was an open-ended question, but to my absolute shock, 56% of customers gave me the exact same phrase.

Are you ready for it? *Be friendly.* That's it. So many customers simply want sales reps to be friendly. Do you know what this means?

It means that many sales reps are *not* being perceived as friendly. This is probably a symptom of being nervous, but you can rise above the crowd by focusing on this. In every single interaction you have with the customer, you should focus on being friendly. Use a warm voice in your calls and emails, use friendly (but not apologetic) tones in your emails, slow down when you speak, and don't be afraid of silence. This is your way of kindly inviting customers to speak so you're not doing all the talking.

Just be friendly. Customers will love you for it.

Customer Insights: Research from Real Customers

How Do Customers Typically Find New Vendors?

In this day and age of unlimited information, between the Internet and social media, customers report they still tend to find vendors the old-fashioned way. More than 70% say that when a need is identified, the best way to bring vendors to the table is to go back to people they already know.

Over half report that they also ask internally and get advice and referrals from inside the organization.

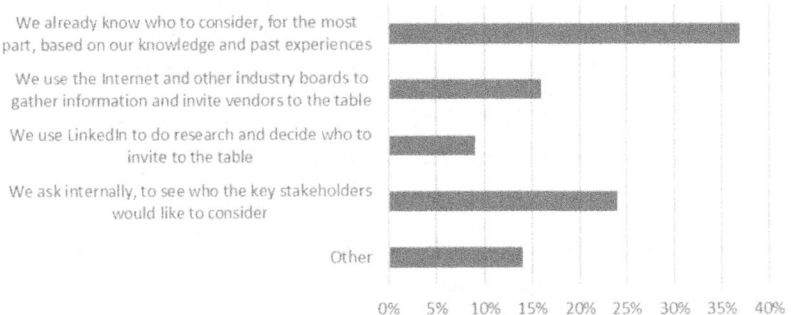

What does this mean for you?

It means that it's your job to stay in front of the customer, on a consistent basis, even if they tell you they don't have a need at that moment. I had one deal where I followed up with the same customer every six months for four years before I ever had a chance to bid on the business.

Eventually, I got the call. They finally had identified a need, and I had established myself as a trusted vendor because of my consistency, and I won that business. Get permission to follow up, and then stick to a schedule, year after year if needed. It will pay off.

THE SALES TIGHTROPE

Four Presentation No-Nos

Customers were asked the question, "What are you pet peeves when someone has been invited in to give you a formal presentation?" The top trends included:

1. Giving your company history. This is a trend that is too common in the business world today. I recall in my early sales days, sitting through a presentation, run by more senior sales reps, where they painstakingly outlined the history of the fetal monitor, dating back to the 1970s. They included pictures. The irony is that we weren't even presenting about the fetal monitor. We just wanted to tell them about it just in case. I remember looking out into the audience during this portion, and the looks on their faces ranged from utter disgust, to confusion, to complete lack of attention. Years later, when I began my research project, my hunch was confirmed: customers *hate* this. They do not care what year you were invented, they do not want to hear about your founding members, and they do not need to know how you have evolved. They do care about themselves and how you're going to make their lives easier. Often, when I teach this concept, I get push-back. People say things like, "But Katie, customers want to know they're working with a reputable vendor. Our history *is* important." The truth is, if the customer wasn't sure if you were reputable, you wouldn't be there. It's your job, in the weeks leading up to the presentation, to encourage them to do their research about you and assure them you're a reputable company. Once that is established, they truly couldn't care less about details. If you want to confirm this, just ask them. They'll tell you.

2. Negative selling. Here we are again. Customers report that sales reps tend to talk about their competitors in the presentation portion of the sales cycle, just as they do during the prospecting call. It's definitely in your best interest to make sure they understand the limitations of your competitor, but *they must be the detective.* They won't believe you, and it just makes you look bad if you outline the weaknesses of their other vendors. You must know your market well enough to know what you can do that your competitor can't, so you can lead them down the path and plant those landmines.

3. Talking about products outside the scope of the project. Most big companies provide a wide variety of products and services. *This is not the time to present the depth of your portfolio.* Customers detest this. Instead, use smaller meetings during your discovery questioning period to find out more about future projects, and if you can, get permission to discuss during the presentation. If you don't have permission, it's not the right time.

4. Saying, "We are the best. We are the only ones who can provide X." Remember what customers care about? Themselves. Not you. Plus, they assume you're lying when you say you're the best or the top-rated. Customers prefer when you stick to their agenda, and to the facts, rather than marketing fluff and lingo.

Does Texting Customers Cross a Line?

An overwhelming 91% of vendors report that they are fine using text to interact with customers. Most say they wouldn't want to use it with a new vendor they've never met and prefer that it's limited to vendors they know. The vast majority of customers (86%) actually report that they really enjoy using text, and that it's their preference, so if you're ever wondering if you should send that text, feel free. However, use common sense. Don't text after hours, keep it short and sweet, and don't send too many. Also, keep in mind that the trail for texts is a lot less reliable than email, so if you are dealing with a sticky situation, and you feel like you need a paper trail to refer back to in the future, stick to email.

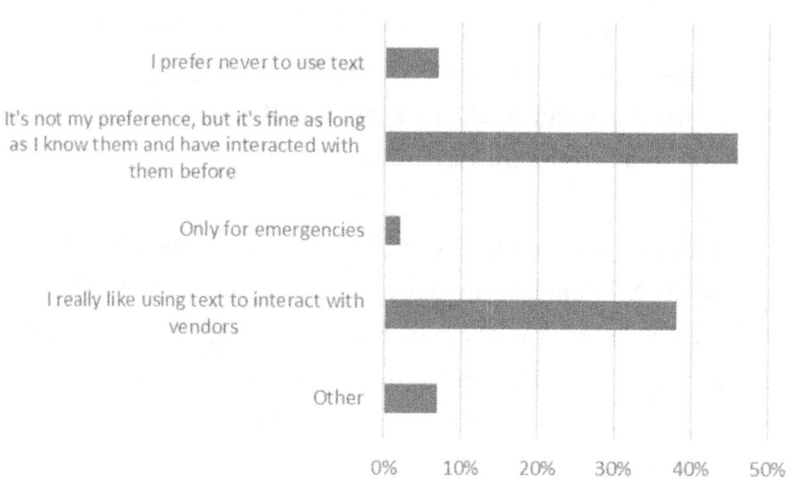

Customer Insights: Research from Real Customers

Do Customers Use TikTok or Instagram to Find New Vendors?

Maybe. Only 20% of customers report that they use social media to find vendors and do their research, and it can be very time-consuming, so it's probably not worth your time. The exception to this is LinkedIn. Customers are *very* active on LinkedIn, and it's well worth your time to learn to use it to your full advantage. However, TikTok, Instagram, and Twitter are probably not worth your time. This will be fairly industry-specific, so if you know you're in an industry where these tools are used more frequently, that is certainly a different story.

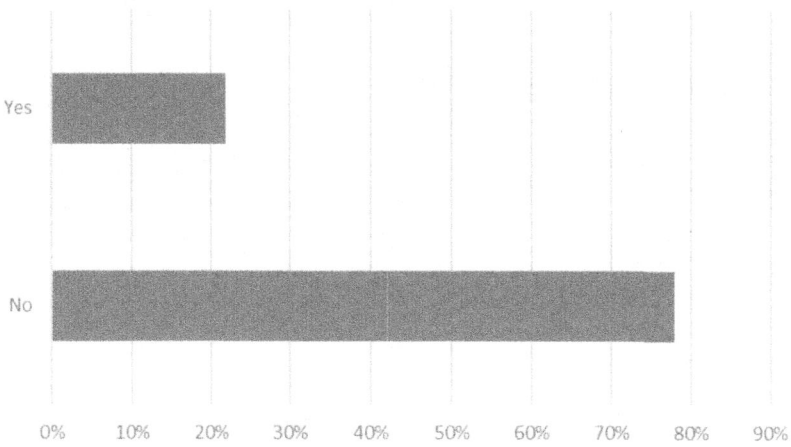

How Often Are Customers Really Getting Contacted by Vendors?

Call reluctance is a real thing. Even experienced sales reps get butterflies when it comes to calling a customer they don't know. Many report they'd rather do anything, even expense reports, than make cold calls. Take comfort in knowing that customers don't get as many calls and emails as you think they do. The vast majority of customers (more than 80%) report that they only get 1–3 phone calls per week, from vendors wanting to introduce themselves.

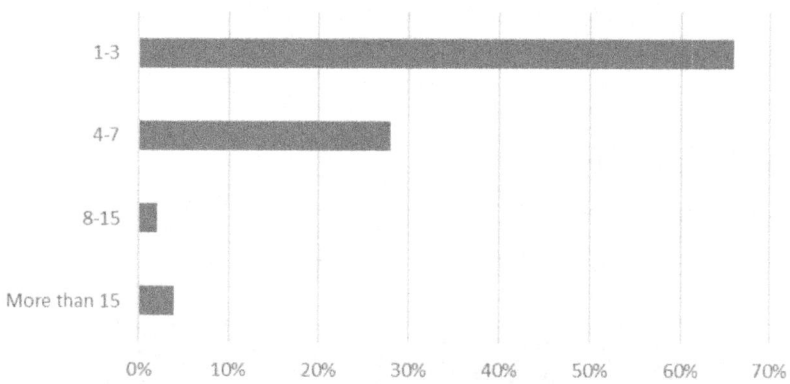

The same is true for emails. Most customers only get 1–5 cold emails per week. Think about how many vendors these people could be getting calls from, and they're only getting a few.

Customer Insights: Research from Real Customers

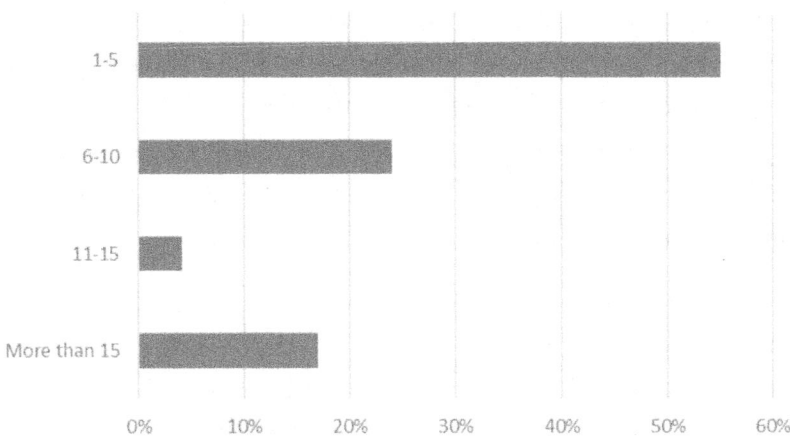

How many cold emails do you get per week on average from someone trying to introduce new products/sell things to you?

The sad truth is that most sales reps are sitting at home, waiting for the phone to ring. If you can force yourself to get into the habit of making calls every week, your funnel will grow. You'll differentiate yourself from other sales reps who might have a lot of momentum when they start their jobs, but then trail off once they win some business. It's just human nature. It's the same reason why gyms are always full at the beginning of January, and by March, everything has dwindled. People lose their steam and fall back into old habits. Don't let that be you. Set a goal to make at least an hour of calls every week, and watch your funnel grow.

Research Conclusions

There is a saying in the sales world that "people buy from people." The idea is that the products don't matter as much as the sales rep, and customers will buy from people they like. This is only partially true. Even I couldn't sell a sub-par product, and trust me, I've tried it. For a period of time, I was selling a product that was under FDA recall and couldn't ship for over a year. Those were dark days.

Assuming you have good products, *now* it's about you. People buy from people, but not just people they like. They buy from people who listen, who are friendly, who seek to understand them, and who are interested in their daily struggles.

Express interest in the customer. They are smart and can tell the difference between genuine interest in them versus genuine interest in making a quota.

Chapter Summary

- Customers don't care about you. Keep it about them and not your company's accomplishments.
- Never bash your competitor.
- Keep picking up the phone. It will pay off as long as you're doing it right.
- During every interaction with the customer, focus on being friendly. If you do nothing else, do this.

Customer Insights: Research from Real Customers

Notes

2

STOP ANNOYING CUSTOMERS: UNDERSTAND THEIR PERSONALITY PROFILE

Once I started my business, I began hosting training seminars. The backbone of the seminar is my customer research and data. Attendees loved digging into the data, but I began to suspect that perhaps some of the power of my customer research was getting a little lost in translation. It was one thing for me to tell my students, for example, that customers hated it when they bashed the competitors, but quite another to hear it directly "from the horse's mouth," as my grandmother used to say.

I decided to host a webinar, and I was able to secure several power players including the CEO of a surgery center, along with the Purchasing Director, the Operating Room (OR) Director, and the Chief Nursing Officer (CNO).

I was excited. It's not every day you get to speak to such a group of important stake-holders, all at the same time.

We had a prep call a few days ahead of time so I could get a feel for the participants and talk through the agenda. I discovered that the CEO was young and eager to get started and also quite outspoken. The Purchasing Director was more soft-spoken and seemed to process information much more slowly. I had a feeling I would have to really work to engage her. The OR Director and the CNO were a mixture of the first two.

The morning arrived for the webinar, and we had a truly enlightening and fun conversation. It lasted for about an hour, and there were many important takeaways. One of the most interesting interactions we had during the entire discussion was when the outspoken CEO shared about her strong preference to avoid all small talk. "Just stick to business," she said. "Don't ask me about my weekend or the weather."

The other panelists did *not* chime in to agree with her, but they also didn't *disagree* with her. After the webinar concluded, I kept thinking about that conversation. Was the CEO right? Should sales reps avoid small talk at all costs? We are usually taught that we need to build the relationship, and thus, we need to get to know the customer and build trust.

I decided to do a little research. I had never studied this before, but now I found that 10% of customers fell into the CEO's category. They hated small talk and wanted to avoid it at all costs.

But that's a fairly small number of customers. Most reported they don't mind small-talk at all, especially if they know the person well. Almost 13% (12.5%) reported they actually enjoyed it and felt like it was an important part of the process.

Stop Annoying Customers: Understand Their Personality Profile

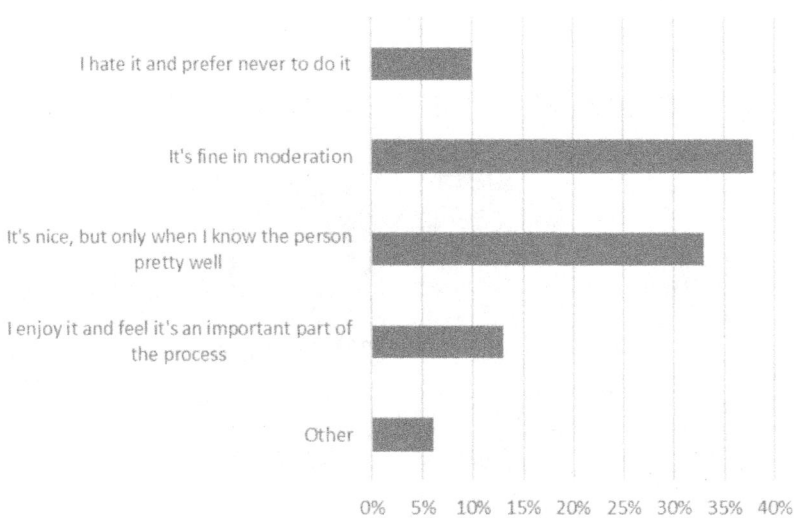

How can we deal with this huge discrepancy in the research? Should we listen to the CEO and avoid small talk? Or should we listen to the majority of customers, who actually like it?

The answer is that customers all have different personalities, and it's our job to decipher them throughout the sales process. How can we do this? By understanding the four different social styles, or personality types.

You might have taken a Myers-Briggs test in the past, or read a book about the Enneagram, especially in the past few years. While all of these personality profiles are fascinating and worthwhile, the most helpful personality profiles in the *sales* arena are the ones defined by David Merrill and Roger Reid, commonly referred to as the Merrill-Reid personality profiles.[1] In the early 1960s, they began researching personalities, from the perspective of the managerial and sales performance angles, and the result is arguably the easiest to understand and the most helpful in terms of defining buyers.

The four personalities they defined include Analytic, Driver, Amiable, and Expressive.

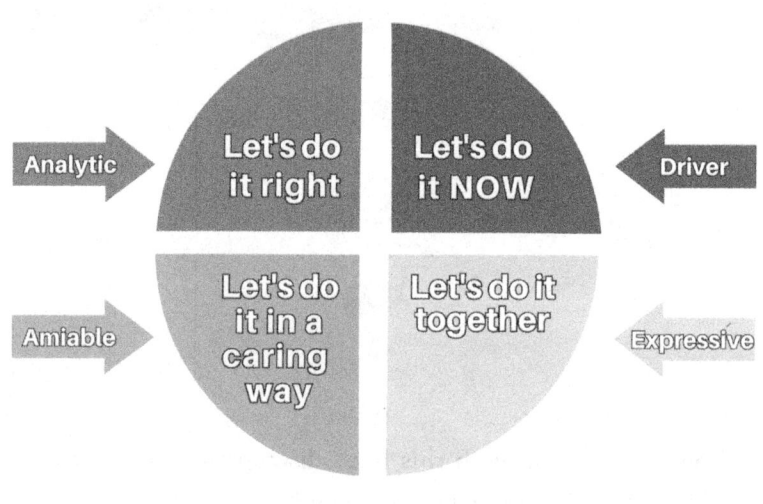

Image Credit: Merrill & Reid

The CEO from my webinar was a **Driver**. She wanted to do everything NOW. Drivers don't want to waste time chatting about the weather. They will be impatient with you if you try to get into the weeds in your explanation or if you use too many charts and present a lot of data. They want the facts and no fluff. They will make quick decisions and move on.

A sales friend of mine once shared about how he was given an hour to present his product. He knew the decision maker well. He knew his team really only had ten minutes to sell to the CEO before he would lose his patience. Perhaps the rest of the team would stick around for the full hour, but the CEO would definitely *not*, and since he was the key decision maker, my friend convinced his team to get the meat of the presentation done first. Although they were skeptical, they agreed. The team finished their presentation in eight minutes, and one minute later, the CEO stood up, announced they had convinced him, and said he needed to get to his next meeting. They won the deal by understanding his personality. My friend later met the CEO's wife and shared the story with her. She laughed and said, "You know him well."

On the opposite end of the spectrum are the *Amiables*. They aren't in a hurry. They hate conflict and enjoy people and relationships. Feel free to ask them all about their weekend plans because they will enjoy building a relationship with you. I was in a meeting once with an Amiable. Somehow we got off track and he started telling me all about his upcoming model train exhibit and competition. Model trains were his hobby, and he was in his element telling me every detail. As a Driver myself, this was excruciating, since I don't like small talk or details. But as a sales rep, it was my job to listen and adapt to his style. Although your friendship might blossom with Amiables, the bad news about them is that they aren't going to be brave enough to push for big changes and would prefer to keep the status quo.

The *Analytics* are also slow-moving, but similar to the Drivers, they are task-focused and won't be prone to chatting. They are the ones who will need all the charts, all of the data, and they will want time to think through every piece of the puzzle. When you meet with them, you might think the meeting went poorly because of the way they interact with others. They also tend to avoid risks.

Lastly, we have the *Expressives*. They are the life of the party. The Expressives hate being alone, love people, and are risk-takers. They will probably talk fast, be charming, and will enjoy chatting with you about their weekend and anything else you find interesting.

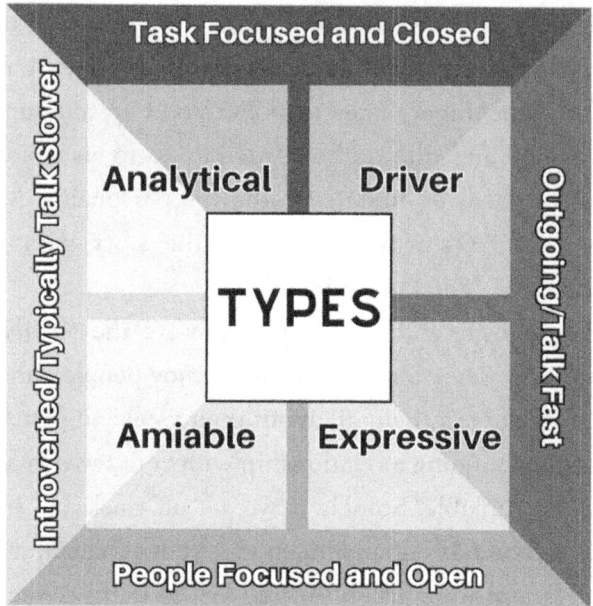

Image Credit: Merrill & Reid

Every time you interact with a customer, start thinking about their personality type, so you can treat them the way *they* want to be treated. Are they an Analytic? Give them lots of charts. Are they a Driver? Get right to the point. Are they an Expressive? Let them talk, and start building the relationship. Are they an Amiable? Never interrupt and don't rush them.

Methods to Identify Different Personality Styles

You might be wondering how you will be able to identify your customer's style. It's not like you can hand them a test and ask them to fill it out before your meeting. It can be a little confusing, but you can start looking for clues right from the beginning.

Stop Annoying Customers: Understand Their Personality Profile

Pay attention to:

- How their voicemail greeting sounds: Are they rushed? Or slow?
- How their gatekeeper treats you and your inquiry: What do they say? Do they ask you to provide lots of details when you send your email?
- How they answer the phone: Do they sound friendly? Or irritated and busy?
- How their office looks: Is it neat and tidy? Does it have lots of decorations?
- What other people say about them: Does anyone internally give you advice on how to deal with them?
- How they write emails: Do they ask *you* about your weekend? Or get right to the point?
- What they write and post about on LinkedIn: This can tell you a lot, if you're lucky enough to have a customer posting on LinkedIn.
- What they comment on and like on LinkedIn: If they aren't posting themselves, you can still see if they're commenting on others' posts, and this will tell you a lot.
- How they speak during a meeting: Do they speak quickly? Decisively? Apologetically?

As you think about your own personality, you might be thinking you sound like both an Analytic *and* an Amiable. This is possible. Humans are complicated, and although the research reveals that most people have one dominant social style, we aren't wholly one way or the other.

When I deliver a training seminar, I ask each member of the team to fill out a short survey that reveals their style. Inevitably, several people are tied. They score exactly the same in two different categories. This is normal and expected and is something you'll have to keep in mind when dealing with customers.

Some will be obvious, such as the CEO in my webinar example, and others will be a little more complicated to understand. Remember, the goal isn't to have them 100% figured out. The goal is to match their style as best you can, so you don't annoy them during the process.[2]

Gaining Their Trust

For every interaction you share with them, think about what you can do to treat them the way they want to be treated, based on their personality style. This applies to emails, presentations, quotes, specs, timing of your messages and follow-ups, phone calls, texts, and everything in between.

For **Drivers**, eliminate small talk. Get right to business. Respond back to them as quickly as possible, and never leave them hanging. They will be ready to make quick decisions, so prioritize their quotes. Keep emails short. You will probably want to limit the storytelling during presentations and meetings. They will most likely prefer texting as a mode of communication.

For **Analytics**, talk slowly. Give them plenty of time to digest the information. Silence is your friend with Analytics. You will need to provide the data, charts, and background information. If possible, you might want to consider bringing in a technical specialist to help answer questions.

For **Amiables**, leave plenty of time for small talk. If you are personally a Driver and small talk makes you uncomfortable, you will want to come prepared with ideas of things you can ask them to sound natural. You will likely need to reassure them of the risk factors in changing to your solution since they are so risk-averse. You might need to keep them on task and make sure you send detailed emails after meetings if tasks were assigned to them. Don't assume you've got the deal just because you seem to get along well with an Amiable. They get along well with everyone.

For **Expressives**, give them space to lead the meeting. They will likely be fun and want to have some laughs. They will want to move quickly, so be ready. They will also probably enjoy using text messages to communicate and will want information promptly. They are going to be slightly impulsive and are more likely to use a "hunch" to make a decision, so be ready to move quickly if they decide that's what they want to do. As with the Amiable, don't assume the deal is won just because they're nice to you. You'll need to dig deeper.

How Can You Make Small Talk if You're a Driver or Analytic?

I am a Driver. In my early days of being a sales rep, I hated small talk, and assumed everyone was like me. I never asked about their family, or their weekend plans, and I didn't realize until later I was missing out on some big opportunities with my closed style of selling.

After I learned about the Merrill-Reid social styles, I forced myself to start making small talk with Amiables and Expressives, but it was never a comfortable thing for me, so I started making a list of things I *could* say. I vowed never to ask anyone about the weather.

If you're like me, and small talk makes you uncomfortable, here are some ideas that won't make you cringe:

- Is this a busy time of year for you?
- Did you have a busy weekend? (*This is better than "Did you have a good weekend?"*)
- How old are your kiddos? (*If you see family photos posted around.*)
- Are Tuesdays usually pretty busy for you (or whatever day you're meeting with them)?
- Have you been in this role for a while?
- Look for any mementos or decorations around their desk area, and see if you can find something interesting to discuss.
- Are you looking forward to _____ (upcoming conference if applicable)?

Put It into Practice

My two children are opposites. One is always in a rush, doesn't like to sit down and chat during meals unless we make him, and he's always creating lists and plans. The other child likes to watch birds out the window for hours and listen to music. Because I know their social styles, I can match my style to theirs in a way that helps out around the house.

As you think through all the people in your life, like your manager, co-workers, friends, customers, spouse, and even your children, you might not want to hand them the quiz you downloaded and demand that they sit down and fill it out, but you *can* start identifying some personality traits. Once you do this, you can start identifying ways you can interact with them in a more positive, empathetic way.

Stop Annoying Customers: Understand Their Personality Profile

One of my favorite parts of delivering my seminars is when we get to the part where everyone has to guess the personality of their manager. I have the management team send in their evaluations ahead of time, and I calculate them, and then at the end of this section, I ask them to guess how their boss scored.

People usually start yelling out opinions, and although there are occasional surprises, they are often right. I have had people come back and report how glad they are to understand their manager better through knowing their personality style. It really does help.

Chapter Summary

- Learn the Merrill-Reid personality styles: Driver, Analytic, Expressive, and Amiable.
- As you interact with customers and other important players in your life, learn to look for cues, such as speaking style, email length and tone, and attitudes of those around them, so you can identify their personality type.
- Once you determine each person's style, adjust **your** style to meet them. Remember to treat people the way *they* want to be treated, not the way *you* want to be treated. Your personality style might be completely different from theirs.
- If you spend the time to understand the social styles, you'll be able to become a truly empathetic and well-liked sales rep.

The worksheet in Appendix A is a great way to keep track of the people in your life to make sure you're categorizing them and putting all this knowledge to good use.

Notes

SECTION II

PROSPECTING FOR NEW BUSINESS: A WINNING FORMULA

3
THE SCIENCE BEHIND WRITING A KILLER EMAIL

By the time I was thirty-five, I had been cooking meals on a daily basis for almost fifteen years. I never used salt and pepper, or really any spices. I didn't think they helped. If a recipe called for Italian seasoning, I would throw it in if I had some, and if I didn't, I would just omit it. My poor husband. Can you imagine how incredibly bland my food tasted? I didn't care. I was too busy taking care of little kids and working a full-time sales job.

I know what you're thinking. My husband could have cooked for himself. And you're right, he could have, but he was in medical school and then residency, and never made it home until after dinner. He would come home to the most bland, tasteless food you can imagine.

Then one day, a neighbor changed my life with scrambled eggs. "Katie," she said. "Cooking without spices is like living life without color. Do you want to live without color?"

I assured her I did not. To prove her point, she cooked two sets of scrambled eggs. In one batch, she omitted the salt, just as I did on a daily basis. On the second set of eggs, she added a small amount of salt.

I was floored. It made a HUGE difference. They tasted *so* much better. She took me shopping for all the spices I had been missing, and from that day forward, I realized how our lives could be improved with a little more flavor. Sure, we were eating food that was nutritious and home-cooked, but every meal could have been SO much better, with a little salt, pepper, and maybe some oregano from time to time.

Writing emails is similar. Everyone knows how to write a basic email, but many people aren't using the spices, so their emails have no flavor. They don't realize how much better and more effective their emails could be if they just used a few different ingredients.

This really came to life when a young sales rep approached me for help with a letter he'd been sending to doctors. He shared that he had tweaked it over and over again, but wasn't getting any responses.

I agreed to take a look, and I found several areas where it could be improved. I didn't change the content much, but I adjusted the subject line, shortened it, created bullet points, and cleared up some confusing statements. I sent it back to him and he called me the next day, absolutely thrilled. Within hours of sending the revised email, he received three replies. This was after *months* of sending out the original letter.

With writing, just a few tweaks can make a **huge** difference. They bring color and flavor to your writing so your customers might actually want to respond.

How to Make Your Emails More Effective

When I do my training seminars, I always ask the question, "Do you know what style of writing receives the best response?"

- Kindergarten
- 3rd grade
- High school
- College and beyond

According to Baydin, the makers of Boomerang, a third grade writing level gets the best response, based on research they conducted on more than five million emails.[1] Why?

Because as humans, we are always trying to conserve energy. Daniel Lieberman writes about this in his book, *The Story of the Human Body*. Back in our caveman days, when we had to find our own food, we couldn't waste even a little energy or we would risk starvation. Our modern bodies are still hard-wired to cut corners so we can save our energy.

> **Smart Email Tip**
>
> Our brains don't want to work harder than they have to. Plus, it's annoying. No one likes words like:
>
> "Synergistic solutions", "Cutting-edge, solid-state technology", "Comprehensive solutions", or "Digital transformations"

Take this email I got last year from a sales rep, trying to sell something to me. Since my LinkedIn profile lists me as the CEO of my small company, I get lots of emails.

Dear Katie,

With that said, I believe that there's an opportunity for X to help you level up your game in expanding your digital roadmap through highly skilled resources who are adequately proficient in cutting-edge frameworks and technologies.

I had (and still have) absolutely no idea what they were trying to sell, and I'm too busy to figure it out. Delete.

You have to write language that's easy to understand. Write the way you would speak to a friend. Avoid fancy marketing language. Here are some email openers that happen too often.

Avoid These	Instead Try
Per our discussion, attached is the quote you requested.	*Great chatting today. I attached the quote for you.*
Pursuant to our discussion...	*Today we talked about...*
I trust you had an enjoyable weekend.	*Hope you had a great weekend!*
I hope this email finds you well.	*Happy Friday!*

5 Elements of a Killer Prospect Letter

There is a science to writing a good letter. Some of the science comes from research from millions of emails sent. Some of it is taking human nature into account. And lastly, some of the science is learned through trial and error. You try something, see what people respond to, and keep track of the winning formula. Follow these steps for writing a great letter, one that will ***actually*** get responses from customers:

Five Steps to a Killer Email

1. According to Salesloft, starting with "Hi, first name" is the best opener for getting a response. It's better than "Dear" or even "Hello."

2. Start with a friendly first sentence. This doesn't need to be fancy or long. I've had many customers tell me, "Just introduce yourself. Plain and simple."

3. Next, mention something about them if you can. This is where you can personalize it and really grab their attention. Do some research. Do they have some old equipment that's almost out of support? Are they hiring a lot of new employees lately, creating some kind of growing pain? If you don't know anything, or haven't been able to find anything from your research, just mention that you'd like to get to know them.

4. Now, give a short bit about your company, followed by brief bullets to summarize what's potentially great about your products/services.

5. Lastly, and this is essential: don't ask them to come up with some times and dates that might work for them. That's too much trouble for them. Tell them you plan to follow up soon and to feel free to reach out in the meantime with any questions. This takes away all the friction and makes it as easy as possible for them to connect with you. It's your job to follow up with a phone call within the week, and if that doesn't work, another email a few days later.

Here's an example of a strong letter that actually gets results, following these steps.

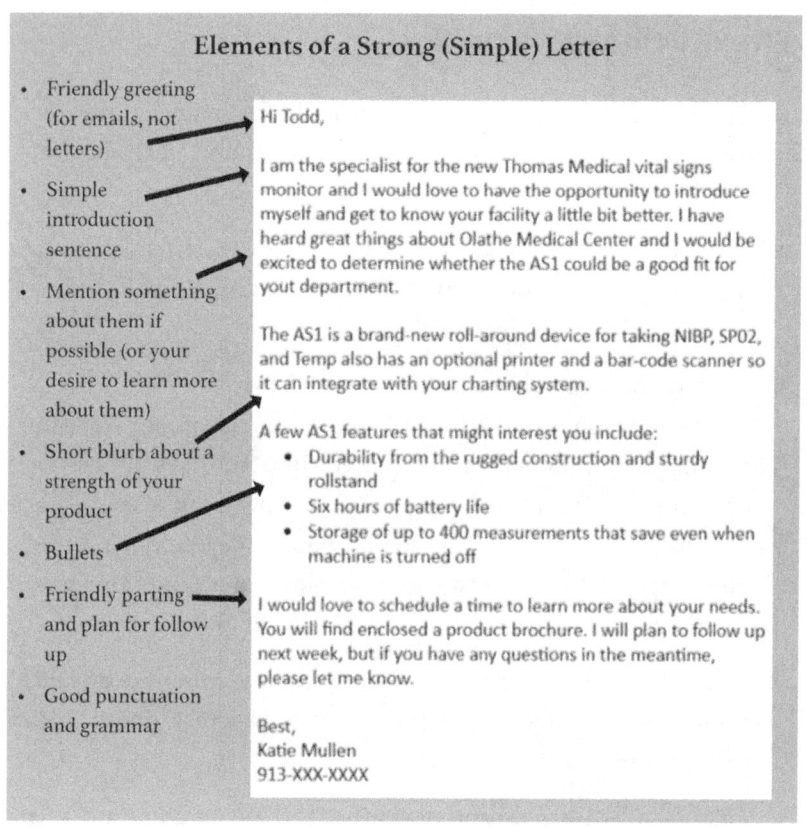

A few other tips for good writing:

- **Keep it short.** According to research from Salesloft and others, 100–300 words is best, or even shorter if possible. Even for internal emails, review and delete any repetitive thoughts. Take out any apologies for bothering them. Delete extra words. Be ruthless with your emails.

- **Avoid hyperlinks.** Any time you include links in your signature line, such as LinkedIn, YouTube, Twitter, your website, etc., you risk getting blocked by SPAM filters. This is especially true if you have lots of hyperlinks.
- **Keep track of what works.** Send at least 25–50 copies of the same email, and keep track of your responses. If you're not receiving replies, tweak something. Change the subject line. Change your bullet points. Keep tweaking until you get a winning combo.
- **Don't beat around the bush.** If they said they were going to get something for you, and they haven't, don't skirt the issue. Just say, "You mentioned you were going to get X for me. I haven't seen it yet, and wanted to see if there is anything I can do to help?"
- **Try sending letters through good old-fashioned mail.** This will really make you stand out, since no one does this anymore. It gives you a reason to call, so that when you do, it's not just a cold call. I have even used this tactic to send thank you notes after a customer makes a big purchase. They really enjoy and appreciate this special touch.
- **Personalize 20%.** This is the sweet spot, according to Salesloft. If you don't personalize at least this much, your read and response rates will be low, and if you do more than 20%, you don't get much out of it, so you've wasted your time.

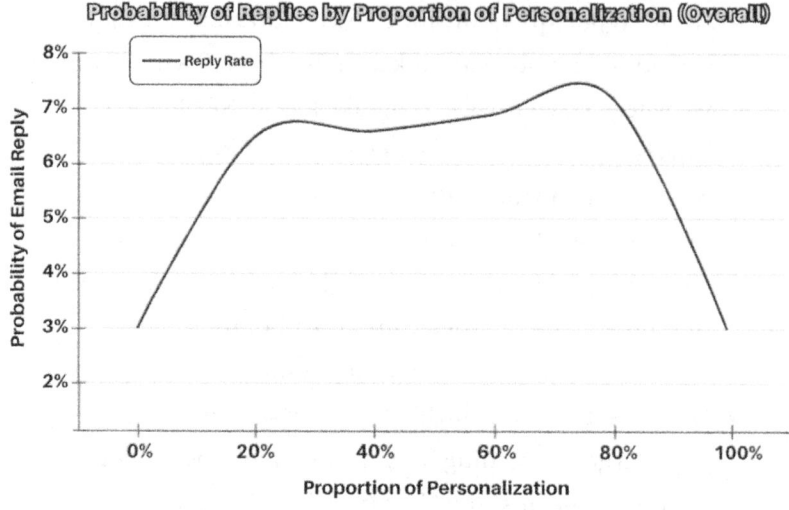

Image Credit: Salesloft

Crafting a Good Subject Line

Once you've got a strong prospect letter, it's time to come up with a good subject line. As with the body of the email, there is a science to writing good subject lines. Research shows you should avoid anything gimmicky, such as:

- "Exciting Promotions"
- "Discounts on X"
- "Do You Want to Save Money?"
- "Can I buy you a cup of coffee?"
- Saying their first name (or your first name)

Keep it short and sweet. Salesloft is a great company that publishes free research on emails and subject lines, and in a study they conducted of more than one million emails, they found that one-word subject lines work best, followed by three words, then two, then four, and once you get past that, things really go downhill.[2]

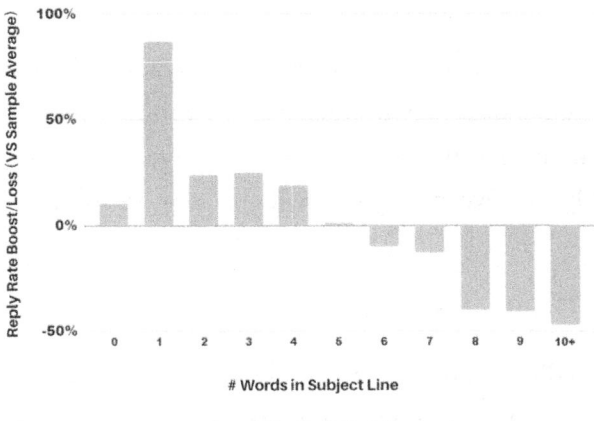

Image Credit: Salesloft

In my own research, I have found that short subject lines generally work well, but here are a few other options I've had success with:

- "Question about X" (X would be your product category, such as monitors, scales, etc.)
- "Follow up on X" (Again, X would be your category of equipment or services)
- "X Opportunity"
- "Ideas for X Support"
- "Meeting"
- Your Company Name (this can be very effective, especially if your company is fairly well known)

The *one* time I've had good luck using long subject lines is when I have already interacted with a person, and I'm waiting on something from them. This is when you know they're busy and probably forgot about you.

For example, let's say a customer promised to get you some specs on their equipment before you can get them an accurate quote. It's been a week, and you haven't heard anything. Try a subject line such as, "Do you have those specs for me?"

And then in the body of the email, kindly remind them that the last time you spoke, they promised to get you the specs, and ask if there is anything you can do to help. I have found this tactic to be remarkably effective, but *never* use it on a new prospect.

Common Grammar Mistakes to Avoid

This is usually the area of my seminars where I get the most pushback. Successful adults don't need grammar lessons, do they?

I'm sorry to tell you that you might be wrong. I estimate that more than 50% of the population consistently makes at least one, if not several, of the mistakes below. Just take a quick look, and see if you can make any adjustments to your daily writing (or speaking). A study from Website Planet found that the bounce rate is up to 85% higher for websites with grammatical mistakes.[3] It would be such a shame to write an amazing letter, only to have someone lose interest because you made a basic error.

On top of that, many sales managers have lamented to me about internal emails. "Katie," they will say, "Can you teach my team to write good emails? I see a lot of bad grammar, emails that are too long, and they even do things like keeping the same email going forever and writing something like 'See below.' Do they really think I'm going to scroll and read back through all that?"

Be the sales rep who stands out by writing succinct, short emails, free of grammatical errors. Your customers and your boss will love you for it.

> **Seven Common Grammar Mistakes**
>
> 1. Incorrect or non-existent punctuation. It makes it harder to read.
> 2. Your vs You're:
>   a. Your is something you own... Your words, your solutions
>   b. You're means "You are." You're welcome.
> 3. There vs. they're vs. their:
>   a. They're means they are. They're very old.
>   b. There is used for "There are several old devices."
>   c. Their shows ownership. "Their old device needs to be replaced."
> 4. ~~Me and Gabe~~ will be coming to the meeting. The correct form is "Gabe and I."
> 5. ~~Her and I~~ will come take a look. "She and I" is how you should write this.
> 6. Irregardless is NOT a word. Use regardless!
> 7. Loose vs. Lose: Loose means a loose screw. Lose means to lose a deal.

You might also consider installing Grammarly. It's an awesome program that lives in the background as you write emails. It also allows you to change your tone for various emails you write. Try the "sound more confident" tone. It's a game-changer for internal emails.

What to Do When They Don't Reply

I often get asked what to do when the recipient just doesn't reply. When is it okay to try again? Should I start a new email? Should I change the subject line?

Here are some tips for you:

- Always try a new subject line. After all, the first one didn't work.
- NEVER start a new email and write that you're following up from a previous email, but provide no additional information. They won't remember you, and I promise they're not going to go back and dig through old emails to find your original message.
- Never send a second email without calling first. Research shows that the most effective way to get in touch with someone is to combine calls with emails. Sending emails alone is 77% less effective than combining an email with a phone call.[4] So, send an email first, then, if you don't hear anything, try a phone call. Then, and only then, you can send another email.
- Never admonish them for not getting back to you yet. So many customers tell me that they get offended when they get an email to the effect of, "I don't know why you haven't replied back to me yet." This is offensive. It's not their job to get back to you. It's *your* job to keep trying.
- After three attempts, start a brand-new email thread, with a totally different email and subject line, and don't reference previous emails. Just start fresh.
- Try sending an Outlook invite. This technique is not for new prospects who have never responded to you. Save this powerful strategy for customers who responded at

some point, showed slight interest, and then went MIA. I can't tell you how many people I have trained who came back and said, "Katie, that totally worked! My customer asked for a quote, and then stopped replying. I sent them an Outlook invite, and they accepted!" Customers are busy people, so to ask them to send you "a few dates and times that work" isn't realistic. With an Outlook invite, they can easily propose a new time, and it makes it as easy as possible to respond.

Timing It Right: When Should You Email?

Your time is valuable. A wonderful mentor once told me, "Katie, you should be fiercely protective with your time." I love the idea that my time is valuable too, even though I'm "just a sales rep." With this in mind, I set out early in my career to be as strategic as possible in everything I do, so I'm not wasting my time.

With emails, timing is important. Don't send emails on weekends. Your reply rates will drop significantly if you do. Know that Mondays are actually the best days to send emails, although there's not a huge difference between Monday and the other days of the week. And the best time of day for all days is around 11 a.m.[5] If you use Outlook, or have a CRM, you can likely schedule your emails to go out at 11 a.m. and on weekdays, to maximize your chances of success.

Chapter Summary

- Use effective subject lines. Play around and see what works best for you.
- Combine emails with phone calls, and other contact strategies, such as LinkedIn.
- Use postal mail to stand out.
- Establish a strategic time for emails.
- Keep it short and sweet.

The worksheet included in Appendix B will guide you through creating killer emails.

The Science Behind Writing a Killer Email

<u>Notes</u>

4

THE ART OF FINDING CUSTOMERS

Last year, I received a random cold call. I was actually on a run, so I don't even know why I answered my phone, but I always respect the hustle of a young sales rep. I was polite, and intended to listen briefly and explain I wasn't interested. To my surprise, I actually thought the software he was selling sounded interesting. I changed my run to a walk and spent thirty minutes on the phone with him. He did an awesome job of listening, asking questions about my business, and explaining how his technology might be able to help me.

He asked if I would agree to join a Zoom meeting to look at the software. I was reluctant. I kind of hate Zoom meetings. I have to get dressed, put on makeup, and sit at my desk and hope my dogs don't bark. I try to avoid Zoom meetings if at all possible, AND I was right in the middle of preparing for an upcoming seminar, but it's hard to get a demo of software without seeing it live, so I finally agreed. I kept an eye out for an invitation from my sales rep, but instead, I got the following email:

Hi Katie,

Thank you for spending some time with me yesterday. John Smith will be taking over from here. He should be reaching out to you soon.

Best of luck,
Alex

What? I was being passed off to someone new? But I liked Alex! He was helpful and knew his stuff. Within a few minutes, I received the following email:

Hi Katie,

I'm looking forward to meeting with you next week. I want to make sure I understand your business, so could you please fill out this quick, 15-minute survey so I can understand your needs? After I get the results, we can set up a call.

Thanks,
John

I quickly responded, and explained that there **must** be some confusion. I'd already spent **thirty** minutes on the phone with Alex, sharing about my business and needs, and could he please get the info from him, as I didn't have time to fill out a fifteen-minute survey?

He wrote back that he preferred I just complete the survey, to maximize our time together. I couldn't believe it. After I stopped what I was doing and ruined my run (which is a sacred time for me!), I was being asked to take **more** time out of my day.

Forget it. My interest was mild at best. I declined the meeting and never spoke with that company again.

This was an incredibly frustrating experience, and I'm not alone. During my research, I discovered that there is widespread disdain for the practice of hiring a call center or junior sales reps to make calls, and then passing the leads along to the local sales reps. It completely destroys the trust you're trying to build. *You* have to be the one to make the calls.

The problem is, many salespeople don't *want* to make the calls. You will hear protests such as, "Why can't someone make these calls for me? I'm way too busy for this. Let's hire a call center or inside sales reps to do the 'grunt work,' and I'll follow up with the leads."

Hearing this tells me one thing about these particular reps: they just want to be order-takers. The problem is that's not really sales, is it? This type of rep is often referred to as a "farmer." They are great at retaining customers, but they never want to hunt for *new* customers.

Don't get me wrong: retaining customers is great, but it's also very, very important to be a *hunter* too. Don't be afraid to get out there and find new customers, and never forget that customers don't like call centers. It ruins the trust we are working so hard to build. The best sales reps are both hunters *and* farmers.

Leads Go Cold Quickly

Not only do customers hate call centers, they're inefficient. MIT Lead Response Management conducted research that included 100,000 inbound leads and discovered that inbound leads go cold within the hour.[1] This means that when you hang up the phone, if John Smith doesn't call the prospect within *one hour* (and really ten minutes is ideal), the chances of actually booking that meeting are slim.

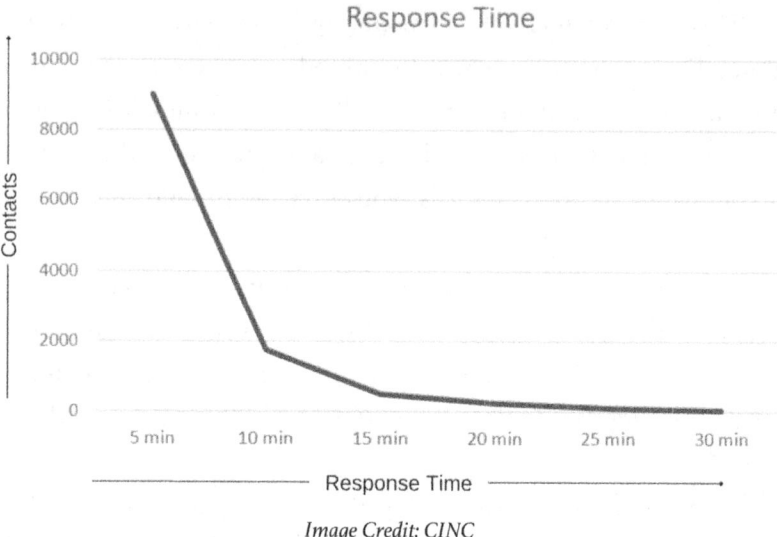

Image Credit: CINC

Most companies are not built to route calls within the hour. I have heard reports of companies taking more than three to four weeks for calls to route to the correct person, and for that person to designate a good time to make those calls. By this time, the calls are colder than a mom sitting at her kid's soccer game in thirty-degree weather. Frigid.

In contrast, if *you* are the one making the call, the lead can't go cold.

Finding the Right Person

Now that you know *you* should be the one making the calls, and that you should prospect often, how do you make sure you're talking to the right person? Many sales reps ask, "Okay, I understand why we can't hire a call center, but can't we at least buy a list of names to save time?"

Yes, it would be amazing to get a list of names on a silver platter, with correct phone numbers and email addresses. Unfortunately, from my experience and research, these lists don't work. The names on the list tend to be old, so when you start calling, you are faced with, "Who are you asking for? She hasn't worked here for years." How embarrassing.

You might be one of the lucky ones, who has a company with an updated CRM database, with all the names and numbers that you need. However, the vast majority of us work for a company with an outdated CRM, which means that we must find the names ourselves. It's the only way to know they're accurate, and it will actually save you time in the long run. Nothing is more frustrating than making your way down an outdated call sheet and completely wasting your time asking for the wrong people.

The Gatekeeper

I vividly remember the day I called a main number for a client and asked for the Director of the Labor and Delivery unit. I waited patiently, and was transferred to Human Resources. I hung up and tried again. Same result.

I thought, "How strange. This person must not understand me." I called a third time. "Hi," I said to the operator. "I think there might be something wrong with the phones. I keep asking to get transferred to the Director of Labor and Delivery, and I keep being sent to Human Resources."

The person on the other end of the phone laughed and went on to explain it was *her* job to screen salespeople. Because I was a sales rep, my only option was to share my information with them, and if the director wanted to talk to me, she would call.

Clearly *that* never happened.

I realized at that moment I had to disarm *everyone*, even the person who answers the phone. Here's an example: I started to experiment, and discovered that if I asked for the **department**, rather than the manager, I got patched right through. Once I got there, someone usually answered, ready to help.

When they did, I'd say, "Hi, I'm Katie Mullen with X Company. I'm calling to introduce some new equipment, and I'd like to send some information to your manager. Can you tell me who I should send it to?" Do you see how non-threatening that is? 99 times out of 100, they will give you the name of their manager, which is exactly what you need, but make sure you get the full spelling of the first *and* last name.

No more blocking or transferring to Human Resources! Now, you sound like you know what you're talking about, and you don't have a big sign flashing above your head screaming, "I'M A SALES REP!!!"

You can also consider trying to get the email address from your helpful phone friend, in case you decide you do want to send an email, too. Unfortunately, if you bluntly ask for it, they will politely inform you that they can't give out this information.

Here are a few ways to get around this:

- Say, "You wouldn't have their email address, would you?" It's non-threatening. Be silent while they figure it out for you. ***Resist the urge to apologize*** for bothering them. Silence is a much more powerful way to get what you want than apologizing or pleading.
- Try guessing their email address. A lot of companies are set up as firstname.lastname@companyname.com. Many companies don't want to share email addresses, or even the format, but you can get around this by going to the company's website, and then to the press release section. That's the *one* place they will usually have an example of how their email addresses are formatted,

and now that you have the full spelling, you just need the email format to be able to figure it out.
- Try using the free tool www.find-business-email.com. I have found that it's not always accurate, but definitely worth a try.
- Lastly, you can try calling the department and saying, "I'm hoping you can help me. I've been trying to send an email to Cindy Smith and it keeps bouncing back, so I must be doing something wrong. I tried cindy.smith@methodist.com, but that keeps bouncing back. Can you help?"

The C-Suite Gatekeeper

My favorite way to get around the C-Suite gatekeeper is to simply wait until after 5:00 to call. Before 8:00 a.m. is also good. Most important people have assistants, but those assistants typically don't like to come in before 8:00 a.m., and they definitely like to leave by 5:00.

This leaves the important person sitting at their desk, answering their own phone. If you call, you just might get them on the line. Holidays are also a great time to call. Labor Day, Memorial Day, and other smaller holidays are days that important people tend to come into the office anyway because it's quieter and they can get more done.

If none of these strategies work, or if you also don't like working after hours (you're in sales and you don't like working odd hours?!), you can try asking for help. Explain that you'd like to get the information in front of the CEO, and ask how others have been successful. Their job is to block you, but they might give you important bits of information if you ask. They might explain that they tend to be on LinkedIn, or that another person is more willing to talk to sales reps. Be humble and quiet, and you'll get some answers.

Making prospecting calls can be daunting, but once you understand the strategy and science behind it, you'll get more comfortable. It can even be fun, once you start having success, and if you use these techniques, you *will* start seeing success.

How to Strategize and Prioritize Your Accounts

You might be feeling overwhelmed about making all these calls, especially if you're new to sales, or have a lot of accounts. Let me fill you in on a little-known secret: Triaging your accounts is your best friend.

First, pull out the "low-hanging fruit." These are the accounts/customers that are the most likely to buy from you. Perhaps you know they are in the market at this moment. Perhaps you know they have liked your company in the past. For whatever reason, they are a good potential customer in the short-term. We will call those your A accounts.

Next, create a category of B accounts. These are less friendly, or have less immediate needs, but they still have good potential.

Lastly, you will identify your C accounts. These customers are extremely *unlikely* to buy from you. They might be on an exclusive contract with a competitor, or have had a bad experience with your company in the past.

If you're not sure how to categorize your accounts, start researching. Ask your internal team. It's possible someone there has already worked with this account in the past, and knows the history. If not, try to get to the gatekeeper and get some basic information and get a feel for how he/she treats you. She might immediately tell you they only buy from X company (your competitor).

Once you have your accounts triaged, it's time to start making calls. But wait! Don't start with the A accounts. You may want some practice, so you should ***actually*** start on your C customers. Keep track of what works and what doesn't, and once you feel good about your strategy and call script, you can start prospecting your A accounts.

Now that you have a solid foundation and you know what's working, you'll really be able to make some traction with your A accounts, but never forget your B and C accounts. Some of my biggest sales have come from C accounts. I was told, "Don't bother. They will ***never*** buy from us. Trust me."

I didn't have enough accounts to write anyone off, so I tried anyway. I methodically called that customer on a schedule, year after year, and my persistence eventually paid off.

Chapter Summary

- Customers find call centers off-putting, so the local sales reps must be able and willing to pick up the phone and make the calls.
- Always be disarming. This is essential with every contact at the facility, even the gatekeeper and receptionists.
- Call lists can be wildly inaccurate, so learning the skills of finding the right contact and getting their name and email will really set you apart.

The Art of Finding Customers

Notes

5

TACKLING THE FIRST 10 SECONDS OF THE PROSPECTING CALL

Now that you know how to find the right person *and* get them on the phone, it's time to figure out what to say. The first ten seconds of a call are crucial. They can determine whether you get screened or get an appointment. In 1988, Neil Rackam published a ground-breaking book called *Spin Selling*. It has become one of the most popular sales books of all time, with over 150,000 copies sold. In it, he conducted extensive research on closing techniques. Conventional wisdom advised sales reps to always ask for the sale. He and others were convinced at the time that to maximize success, a sales rep needed to "Always Be Closing" (the old ABC method), so he set out to prove that if sales reps were given training on *how* to close, they would be much more successful in their closing rates.

He found the opposite to be true. He was almost reluctant to present his research because, at the time, he knew he was going completely against the norm, and he worried about how people would react.

This began the eternal debate in sales of the "hard close" versus the "soft close." The truth is, what Neil and his team had stumbled upon is that customers hate the hard close. They hate to be pressured into making a decision. They perceive it as pushy, and it's one of their top pet peeves.

I think you can take Neil's findings a step further and surmise that customers also don't like a "hard opener" during those first ten seconds. Customers despise it when sales reps open with something like, "Hi, my name is Katie Mullen and I'm calling from X company. We have a new promotion right now that you might really like. It's for our new X machine, which has cutting-edge technology for your clinical needs in the ER, and can end up saving you time, money, and…"

Are you bored yet? Customers are, and it sounds so pushy. I get many sales calls since I'm listed on LinkedIn as the CEO, and I have had sales reps call me and talk for over two minutes before taking a breath. Two full minutes.

Here are some openers that are too aggressive:

- "I'm calling to offer you our limited-time discounts on our XYZ products, and I think you'll really want to take advantage of this, because…"
- "My name is Katie Mullen, and we at XYZ company won the XYZ award for the fifth year running because of our cutting-edge products that…"
- "I'm calling because I am confident I can save you money, and I feel confident you'll want to take advantage of all the savings we can offer…"

These openers will make the customer immediately defensive and give the impression that you're being one of those "pushy" sales reps they hate so much. Instead, we need to disarm them and make them feel safe. Start building that trust by keeping your opener soft and non-threatening.

Customers really do hate this pushy, forced approach, and here's your proof. Read through these quotes, heard directly from customers during my research:

- "I hate when they believe they understand my struggles or assume technology gaps, but they really don't."
- "They tell me when they are going to be meeting with me rather than asking me when a good day/time is."
- "I hate when they jump right into it and don't ask if now is a good time. I frequently am in a meeting, so I get frustrated when they just get into it and don't give me a chance to tell them it isn't a great time."
- "The biggest pet peeve is a vendor not coming quickly to the point with a clear message as to the purpose of the call."

We need to give them space to think and respond to you. You might be thinking, "Okay, I know what *doesn't* work. But what does?" Try one of these:

- **"Hi Mike, this is Justin with X Company. Are you swamped?"** This is my favorite opener. It's short, which is ideal. Also, it gives them a chance to talk. You can figure out what kind of mood they're in. Are they irritated? Busy? Friendly? Then you can act accordingly. Plus, customers like to say the opposite, so instead of asking (as most people do) if it's a good time, try asking if it's a **bad** time, or my preference, ask if they're swamped. Usually, they will reply with something along the lines of, "No, I mean, kind of, but it's fine. Go ahead."

- "Hi Mike, this is Justin with X Company. I wanted to follow up and see if you got the information I sent." I like this one because it's not quite a cold call if you do it this way. You're following up on something, so this can be a really good one if you're a new sales rep. It takes away a little of the pressure because you have something to talk about. Also, customers really like this. Many customers said during my research that they preferred when sales reps sent information before calling, so they had time to review it.

- "Hi Mike, I wanted to call and introduce myself. I'm Justin, and I'm your X Company support person." (Pause here, see if they say anything.) If not, then... "I'm calling because we have some new equipment you may not have seen." (Pause.) "Is that anything that's been on your radar at all?" Do you see how I paused? It gave them time to get you off the phone quickly if needed. That's one of the best ways to start building trust. And I love asking them if something has been on their radar. It's a great way of finding out what's been on their mind and whether anyone within their staff is talking about it. I find that many times, the reason a manager will be interested in equipment or services is because their staff has been complaining about the current solution. When you ask if something is on their radar, it's a nice way of asking if their staff has complained lately.

- "Hi Mike, this is Justin with X Company. This is a cold call (laugh), so I understand if you want to hang up, but I'd love to take a few minutes to explain why I'm calling and see if you're interested." This one isn't my personal favorite, but the guys over at 30 Minutes to

President's Club Podcast have had great luck with it and highly recommend it, so if you feel like it's your style, give it a shot.[1]

The common theme in all these soft openers that actually work is that they're short, and they depend on you being silent after you speak. Resist the urge to fill the silence. It's awkward. I know it is. As humans, we want to avoid silence, especially with strangers, but we absolutely MUST let them fill that silence. It shows them we're *not* pushy, that they can trust us to let them off the phone if needed, and it allows *them* to do the talking, which is essential at the beginning. Your customer does not care about you. *Yet*. They might eventually, but for now, your job is to remember that the customer does not care about you.

Keep It Casual

One reason so many of these openers work is because they're conversational. They aren't formal and full of marketing fluff. Humans are always trying to conserve their energy, and customers are incredibly busy people. If you sound *at all* like a telemarketer, customers will be done with you.

Stay away from phrases like, "Our records indicate," or "As you may be aware."

Often, when I work with companies, it turns out that their marketing or even engineering team has written the call script they're trying to use. They are often full of phrases that might be seen on a marketing brochure, instead of in a conversation. Take this example:

> "With X Company, our systems provide safety first and offer savings potential, ease of use, and a maintenance plan. All

of this comes with our streamlined installation process managed by a dedicated team of experts. We also have a special, introductory, limited-time promotional program designed for you and your staff. Could we set up a time for us to bring it in and show you? Maybe next Thursday?"

People don't talk like this. No one says, "I have a special, introductory, limited-time promotional program."

In real life, a person would say, "We have a deal going that might save you money." (Although I never recommend starting with this. They won't care about your special deal unless they actually want to buy from you, which won't happen until much further down the road in the sales process.) Pretend you're talking to a neighbor who asks you what you do for a living and why someone would buy from you.

Avoid These	Instead Try
"Our records indicate you have an X device."	"It looks like you guys had an X device. Do you know if that's still around?"
"I'm calling on behalf of X Company."	"My name is Katie from X Company."
"I'm calling to see how we might be able to better assist you moving forward."	"I'd love to see how I might be able to help you. I'm sure you have a decent amount of our old equipment, and sometimes you might not know where to go for help."

Tackling the First 10 Seconds of the Prospecting Call

Be Friendly

Think back to what customers said when I did my research. The biggest piece of advice they gave to sales reps? Be friendly.

The question is, how do we do that without acting *too* friendly over the phone? Customers report that they also don't like it when sales reps act like they're best friends. Try some of these techniques:

- Stand up and smile while you're talking on the phone to a customer.
- Be a great listener. Never, under any circumstances, interrupt them.
- Use the PAUSE. Awkward silence is perfectly fine and preferable in sales. Let the customer fill that awkward silence, and they will automatically find you friendlier.

Timing and Cadence

When and how you call is just as important as being friendly and keeping it casual. Maximize your time by calling on the most effective days. Do you know what day that is? Wednesday. Then Thursday. CallHippo released this data after they researched thousands of calls.

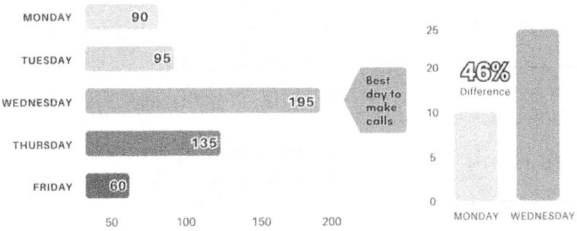

Image Credit: CallHippo

What about timing? Morning is best (either 11:00-12:00 or 8:00-9:00), followed by late afternoon (between 4:00 and 5:00).[2]

Let's go beyond this basic research. Think about the lives of your target audience. Do they typically get into the office super early? Do they have the type of job where they sit at their desk when they first arrive? Or will they be running around doing stuff for the first few hours?

If you're in the medical device field, you might know that nurse managers are usually doing rounds and not at their desk for the first few hours, so don't try them at 8:15. Give them until mid-morning.

Biomeds (the ones who take care of broken equipment) tend to arrive early, sometimes by 6:00 or 6:30 a.m. They love getting calls that early. One of my biggest sales came at the beginning of my career, and it all originated from a 6:30 a.m. call I made to a Biomed. He shared with me that no one called that early, and he really respected my hustle. We booked a meeting, and it all took off from there.

The reason it worked is because I respected his schedule and I put myself in his shoes. Think through your customers' daily lives and decide when might be the best time of day to call. Once you've made the decision, make it a weekly habit.

Send yourself an Outlook invite, and hold that time sacred. Know that you can't book any meeting for Wednesdays from 9-10 a.m. because that's your prospecting hour. Feel free to book yourself more time, but make it a minimum of one hour per week. You'll be amazed at how many deals you start putting in the funnel if you do this consistently—which keeps your boss off your back. Yay!

Now let's think through your prospecting strategy. Are you in the habit of *only* sending emails? Do you send out twenty emails to prospects and call it a day without ever picking up a phone? If so, you're not alone. We've all experienced call reluctance. It can be daunting and annoying to make those calls. However, if you're *only* sending emails, you're going to be 77% less effective. If you're *only* making phone calls, you're going to be 91% less effective.[3] It's all about the multi-contact strategy, which combines email with phone, voicemails, LinkedIn, and appointments with other departments.

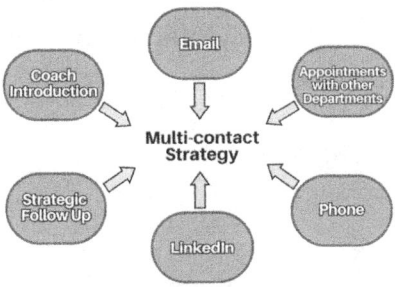

You will be more effective if you vary the cadence. Cadence refers to the flow and days between calls and emails.

Let's say you've identified a great prospect. Maybe she is the director of your ideal department.

Step One: Call and use your disarming methods to find out her name (and how to spell it). Send her an email you've carefully crafted.

Step Two: Assuming no response, you wait four days, then you send an email, followed by a phone call a day later.

Step Three: If you still haven't gotten a response, wait a week, and then call. If she doesn't answer, leave a voicemail this time (even though we know she probably won't respond).

Have you counted your touches (attempted interactions)? We're up to four by now.

Should you give up now? No way! Do you know how many touches you typically need to make before you get a response? If you make at least six attempts, you'll be more than 80% more likely to get connected.[4]

The crazy thing is, many sales reps give up after the first call. Keep going, and you'll separate yourself from everyone else. Vary the methods of connection and the numbers of days in between attempts until you connect.

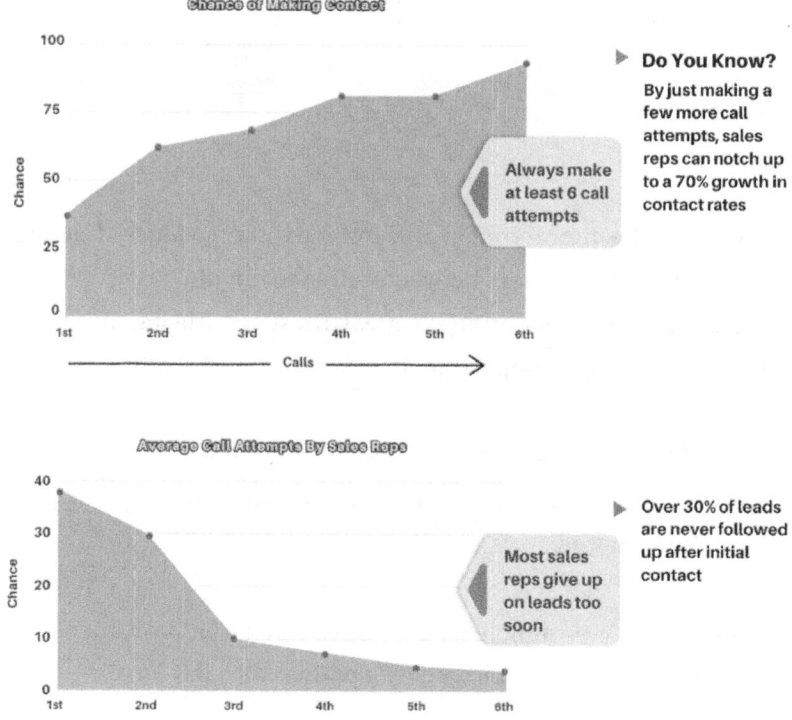

Image Credit: CallHippo

Tackling the First 10 Seconds of the Prospecting Call

The name of the game is *polite persistence*. One of these days, you will call, and BAM! She will answer. She will say she's received your emails and messages and knows what you're calling about. She will say she's not ready to talk yet, but is planning to budget next year, so call her back in January.

Now you've started building trust, and you have permission to call back. That's a major win: polite persistence paid off.

Talk Tracks/Scripts

Should you make a call script? Is it worth your time? Most people are reluctant, because they are worried about sounding like a telemarketer (and because they aren't that fun to put together... expense reports anyone? That would probably be more enjoyable than putting a call script together from scratch!).

But, they *are* important. They help you not veer off and make an unnecessary mistake. If you practice enough, especially in front of a mirror, while walking around and smiling, it will sound natural. Call scripts don't make you sound canned. They make you sound prepared and professional. Do actors "wing it" when they work? Would you "wing it" when giving a presentation? I would hope not. So don't wing it with prospecting.

Voicemail Strategy

As with so many things in sales, there is an art to leaving a good voicemail. The best voicemails are:

- **Friendly/Warm** - Work on this at home. Smile while you talk. Try it a few times by leaving yourself a voicemail to see how you sound. You might be surprised at how cold you sound when you don't try.

- **Short** - Resist the urge to keep talking. What you're tempted to say in the voicemail, write in an email instead. Voicemail is NOT a place to communicate important information. Just say your name, your company, and your phone number. Mention you will send an email to follow up, and then hang up. The shorter, the better.
- **Slow** - When we get nervous, we talk fast. Force yourself to slow down and enunciate all your words.

A great strategy is to tell them you're going to send information (or that you already did). Don't bother asking them to call back. They won't, as we learned in my customer research. If you try this strategy, make sure you send the email right away. It's tempting to batch emails and send them all at the end of the day, but if they listen to your voicemail in the middle of their day, and feel mildly interested, they're much more likely to respond if they get the email right away, before they forget about you.

Remember, too, that people go on maternity leave. (I have! Twice!) They take medical leave. You won't know this unless you listen to the entire voicemail message when a customer doesn't answer. They might be telling you they're going to be out of the office for eight weeks, and that you should try someone else, so listening to the entire voicemail message is crucial.

The Best-Kept Secret to Prospecting

After a few years of using these strategies, I won the "Pinnacle Award." This means I got to travel to an exotic destination with 150 of my best work pals and chat about work while wearing my swimsuit.

When I got back, I started making calls again. My goal was to

Tackling the First 10 Seconds of the Prospecting Call

make it to Pinnacle again, and the only way I knew how was to keep prospecting week after week. Shortly after, I got a call one day from my Account Executive. We called on the same accounts, but sold different products. He asked me if I had just gotten off the phone with a particular customer.

I thought I was in trouble, so reluctantly admitted that I had. He laughed and said, "Wow. I thought since you just got back from Pinnacle, you'd slow down a little. I guess I was wrong. Good for you. I guess that's why you'll probably always be at the top."

The truth is, it's pretty easy to be successful in your first few years of sales. You're full of energy and excitement. Once you learn the process and gain momentum, sales come easily. It's years later that really show what you're made of. If you want to not just be successful one year, but for your career, you'll keep making those calls, week after week. It must become a habit.

No one teaches habits better than James Clear. In his best-selling book, *Atomic Habits*, he illustrates that for habits to become permanent, they must be easy. Take away all the friction you can from making those weekly calls.

Maybe try a new location, such as your kitchen table or even your car, so you're not tempted to check your email or clean off your desk. It doesn't seem like cleaning off your desk will be more appealing than a task like making calls, but you never know. Customers can be brutal.

Program all the main numbers of your customers into your phone. It'll be easier than having to look them up every time.

Next, be specific. Identify exactly when and where you will begin your prospecting habit and how long your session will be, and send yourself that recurring appointment request to hold yourself accountable.

Establishing these habits will pay off, and next thing you know, *you'll* be the sales rep going to Pinnacle every year.

Chapter Summary

- Soft openers work better than aggressive, hard openers. Always disarm the customer.
- Keep it casual. Don't use fancy words, and never start your call promising to save them money or talking about a promotion. They must be interested in your product before they care about the price.
- Leaving voicemails isn't always effective, but if you do leave a voicemail, make sure it's short and warm. Resist the urge to give lots of details here and follow up quickly with an email.
- Be prepared with talk tracks. Know what you're going to say.

The sample script included in Appendix C will help you craft an amazing customer call script.

Tackling the First 10 Seconds of the Prospecting Call

Notes

6

UNCOVERING PAIN POINTS USING THE MAGIC WEDGE QUESTION

Jeff Maxwell had always been a super social kid. In middle school, he played football, basketball, and ran track. He was always begging his mom to drop him off at the park to play with his buddies. He would be out for hours, throwing the football around and hopping from house to house, looking for more friends to join the fun.

But freshman year of high school was a different story. That's when he became what his mom considered "anti-social." Instead of going out with friends on the weekends, he preferred to stay home playing video games by himself.

Week after week, his mom asked him why he didn't want to go out with friends. "What about Johnny, Max, and Kevin?" she asked. "You guys always had so much fun together, I don't understand why you don't want to hang out with them anymore."

Jeff just shook his head, not even lifting his eyes from his game. "Just text them!" his mom urged. "I'm sure they'll invite you to come along if you just ask."

Jeff always ignored her. Week after week, he told her he didn't care what they were doing, and didn't want to go anywhere. Her worry grew, until she finally demanded he see a therapist for his depression.

Only then did Jeff confess the truth. He didn't want to go out with his friends because they had all started drinking and doing drugs. He didn't want to tell his mom because he didn't trust her. He was worried she would call their moms and tell them everything. It turns out he wasn't actually depressed or anti-social. He was just a good kid, trying his best to stay out of trouble.

In sales, customers are like teenagers. They don't want to tell us their secrets because they feel threatened and don't trust us. Yet.

We must earn their trust first, so they are willing to share their secrets. We can earn their trust by being friendly, respecting their time, and asking questions.

And, just like teenagers, we can't assume we know what's going on with them. Just because one customer has experienced certain problems doesn't mean every customer will share the same set of problems. Every customer is different.

This was never more clear to me than early in my sales career when I made a big mistake. At the time, I was selling patient monitors, and everyone wanted to connect directly to the electronic charting system. It was a gaping hole in our offering that we didn't connect to the EMR system.

One day, they announced that we had FDA clearance and could now connect. I was thrilled! I ran around the tri-state area, telling anyone who would listen about our amazing new feature.

I had no idea it was about to come back and bite me. I was visiting a customer I had always wanted to land. He asked me the inevitable question: "Can you connect to our charting system?"

I excitedly responded that we absolutely could! I went on to tell him all the detailed specs, just to impress him, but he interrupted me. "Katie, wait. We actually tried that with your competitor, and it didn't work out at all. We hated it. Sorry, I don't think this is the product for us."

Wait, what? He said he didn't want our amazing new technology that we'd worked so hard for? This can't be happening!

I did my best to back-track. I explained that it was only an option, and wasn't a requirement, but the damage was done. "Sorry, Katie," he said. "I think your product is just too complicated for us. We need something simpler."

I learned an important lesson that day. When he asked if we could connect to the charting system, I shouldn't have *assumed* that he wanted to. I should have responded with, "Is that something that's important to you?"

He would have told me all about the trouble they had in the past, and I would have learned exactly what I needed to know to win that deal. I would have learned that I needed to focus on the simplicity of the technology and how easy it was to operate.

If you can focus on gaining trust so the customer feels comfortable sharing, and take the time to listen and never assume you know what they're going to want, you will truly stand out from the crowd.

Secrets Revealed

So how do we get their secrets? First, we don't interrogate them. I did a podcast a few years ago with the head of purchasing for a fairly large hospital. He said he sometimes felt like vendors put him in the hot seat, like he was getting interrogated under a bright light, which he didn't like.

He said they asked him all kinds of invasive questions about how the process worked, how it would get approved, who would be making the final decision. Does that help the customer? No.

It helps you and your boss and your management team

because, with that information, you can accurately put together a forecast. This will definitely win you points with your boss, but it does not help the customer at all. They see this as a waste of their time and they see it as a self-serving act.

I often see sales teams being told that they should lead with one of the following:

- Promotions
- Warranty info
- An offer to build a quote with your pricing
- Statistics on how your products work/facts about product performance
- Questions about timeline, budget, decision makers, etc.

Do you see what all these have in common? They're about *you!* And what is the one thing customers don't care about? You.

Instead of worrying about you and your company, we start by disarming, as we learned in the previous chapter, and then we ask good questions that show we are interested in the *customer's needs*. Lastly, you frame up your solution.

If you skip ahead, and frame your solution before the other steps, you won't get the information you need to win the deal. I often hear people asking me how to close deals, how to overcome objections, and how to overcome a competitor undercutting you on price.

The truth is, if you do the first two parts correctly, you won't have many objections, and you can convince them that your value outweighs the fact that you're more expensive. That's the beauty of this method. It helps you avoid issues at the end, so that closing is a breeze.

Think back to my example about the customer who wanted simple monitors, not complex technology. That is a classic example of skipping steps. I skipped to step three too early, and see what happened? I put myself in a terrible position.

The best salespeople don't skip steps in this process. No one wants to have a meeting with a sales rep who immediately starts talking about themselves and their products. Don't show up and start with step three.

Pre-Call Data Gathering

My kids are in middle school, and there are all kinds of things they don't like about school: the dress code, the morning start time, the amount of homework they're given. I always tell them to choose their battles. If you ask for everything you want, you'll probably get nothing.

But if you pick your battles, you just might get what's most important to you. Customer meetings are similar to this. Before you even get in front of the customer, there are steps you can take to gather basic information. Customers are only going to answer questions for so long, so it's vital that we pick our battles and choose our questions wisely before they get impatient and tell us they're finished.

If you consider that we will only get 5–10 questions maximum in that first meeting, we can't waste time asking about information we could have researched ahead of time, such as:

- What is their business
- What is their buying group (if any)
- Their budget cycle (Someone within your organization should know this. If not, save the question for the end, once they've asked for a quote and seem comfortable with you.)
- What keeps them up at night (Strike this from your vocabulary. No one ever wants to be asked this question.)

You can gather great information from LinkedIn, their company website, internal reports, internal CRM database, and fellow sales reps who might have already sold to them at one point or another. If you've already been in the facility, check around and see if they have posters on the wall with mission statements, goals, or any other useful information about what's important to them.

Art Sobczak does a great job covering this concept in his book, *Smart Calling*. He argues that we shouldn't "cold call." We should always be making a "smart call," and this is accomplished by:

1. Taking a little bit of time to prepare and understand the customer
2. Using that information during your call to have a consultative (but informal) conversation
3. Providing value to the customer in some way moving forward

Uncovering Pain Points Using the Magic Wedge Question

The wisdom of this approach was perfectly illustrated during a podcast I did with Chris Nowak, a Corporate Director of Healthcare Technology Management and Integration. A big part of his job is dealing with vendors, and he shared that one of his biggest pet peeves is when a sales rep comes in completely unprepared and doesn't even understand his basic business.

He urges sales reps to do a little homework before they waste his time. The time you put in will pay off, but make sure you don't spend hours on this. A little background information goes a long way, and you can find yourself going down a rabbit hole if you're not careful, preventing you from making your call.[1]

Disarming Them

We learned how to disarm the gatekeeper so they will give you the name of the manager, and now it's time to disarm your customer to get them talking.

Think of this like the part where you disarm your teenager. Instead of demanding to know why he's been so cranky, you offer him cookies and gently say, "You're not acting like yourself lately. Is everything okay?" Trust me, this is a much more effective way to get information out of teenagers. Customers are the same way. We can't come in aggressively and demand information.

Great disarming questions to get things rolling can look like this:

- **"What do you guys use now for X equipment?"** The trick to this question is to let them talk. They might offer a bunch of information just from this first question. If not, at least you don't sound pushy.
- **"Is that pretty new?"** This is a great question. This is one of those I stumbled across by accident, and was

amazed to discover how effective it was, so I kept using it. People like to say "no" to sales reps. It's reverse psychology. If you said, "Will that need to be replaced soon?", they will be on the defensive and will want to tell you why it doesn't need to be replaced. With this question, you'll get a real answer, and maybe, if you're patient, they'll volunteer whether or not they plan to replace it anytime soon. Be silent, and let the magic happen.

- **"That's working out pretty well?"** Again, this is the magic of reverse psychology. You're putting them at ease. You're inviting them to open up about all things they dislike about their current products/services. If you'd asked them to tell you what they didn't like about their current solution, they would feel the need to defend. This is like giving them a warm batch of chocolate chip cookies. It opens the dialogue, and before you know it, they'll be spilling their secrets about everything they dislike. Make sure you give them space to expand here. Let silence work for you and resist the urge to fill it.
- **"Oh?"** This is one of my favorite phrases of all time, which I learned from Smart Calling. It's the same thing as saying, "Tell me more," but less desperate. Just utter this phrase, and let silence ensue. You'll get a goldmine of information.
- **"Is new equipment on your radar at all?"** The phrase "at all" is very disarming. It softens anything you have to say. Now that you've gotten them talking about how old their equipment is, and what they don't like about it, it's time to move things along by asking this non-threatening question.

Uncovering Pain Points Using the Magic Wedge Question

As you think about disarming the customer, it's important to remember that disarming a customer does *not* mean asking about the weather, asking about their weekend, and making small talk. Remember, this would only work with Expressives and Amiables, and might build the relationship with the right people, but doesn't move a sales conversation forward.

Don't make the mistake of beating around the bush as a way to disarm. Customers don't want to have a vague conversation that seems to be leading nowhere. You'll still want to ask your questions, just in a softer way at first.

Since you're asking questions in a soft way, you'll find that customers are talkative. Once they're warmed up, it's time to really get some information. To do this, we'll move to step two: the wedge questions.

The Wedge Question Explained

In *SPIN Selling* by Neil Rackam, he introduces the concept of Implication Questions. These questions move beyond the basic qualifying questions, such as the budget and decision-makers—which is what most sales reps start with—and help uncover potential problems the customer is experiencing. If done well, you will uncover all their secrets: the exact secrets you need to know in order to frame up your solution beautifully. I will refer to these questions as *wedge questions*.

You might remember the triplet example from Chapter One. In that example, the sales rep was selling to a high-level trauma center, and was knowledgeable enough to know that they likely *did* deliver triplets from time to time. Instead of just stating the facts: "We can monitor triplets, isn't that great?", the sales rep asked the question: "Would it ever be important to have a device to monitor triplets?" This is an example of a *wedge question*.

The beauty of this is that it's specific enough to open up a possible pain point. It's not a vague question. We're not asking, "What keeps you up at night?" or "What's important to you in a fetal monitor?" None of those questions will get them talking. The customer will probably just answer that they are fine with their current monitor, and they sleep fine at night, but thank you anyway.

The wedge question is your secret weapon to discovering what *is* important to them. We "wedge" ourselves in there, and ask (in a disarming way) about specific pain points they might have. The goal here is to start a nice, fruitful discussion. Interactive meetings with customers are more effective than a lecture or PowerPoint presentation.

A real-life wedge question might look something like this. You show up to a car dealership with your two small children. They're running wild, and everyone is looking at you as if to say, "Get your kids under control, lady!"

A smart salesperson would observe the children and immediately know what wedge questions to ask. First, he would ask what kind of car you currently drive, and when you replied a small SUV, would then ask, "Do you ever have trouble with your car doors slamming into the cars next to you as the kids get out?"

The stressed-out mom would reply, "Yes, it happens all the time!" and go on to tell story after story, all while the sales rep listens attentively for other information that might create more wedge questions. He'll eventually suggest that she look at a minivan with sliding doors that **don't** slam into the car next to you, and even have a button to open and close. Problem and frustration solved!

The reason wedge questions work is because we can discover what's really important and what's **not**. It's certainly possible that this particular mom could have had a rule that the children aren't allowed to open the doors, no matter what. In that case, she might not care about the sliding doors as much, so the salesperson could have moved along to something that's more important to her. Not every mom is the same, and not every customer is the same.

That's why we don't just come in and tell them about all of our amazing features. They might not care, and then we will waste valuable time and bore the customer. Wedge questions help us figure out what we should *eliminate* when we frame up our solution.

Creating *Your* Wedge Questions

The most important thing about wedge questions is that we remember the goal is to move the sales process forward **to our advantage**. To craft a quality wedge question, we will start with our unique competitive advantages. These are things that make us truly different. They can't just be, "our outstanding customer support."

To get your list of unique competitive advantages, imagine asking an existing (and happy) customer for examples of how *your* product has made *their* life easier. What would they say?

You can also try talking to the person who trains the staff on how to use your products, if you have one. They typically really know the customers *and* the products. What do customers ask them for? When they spend time doing the training for new products, what truly excites them after the installation? This is how you identify your unique competitive advantages.

Consider this fictional example. On the left are unique competitive advantages. On the right is the corresponding wedge question.

THE SALES TIGHTROPE

Competitive Advantage	**Wedge Question**
8 hours of battery	"Is battery life *ever* an issue?"

They might have them plugged in all the time, so they might not care about battery life, no matter how great it is.

4-hour recharge	"Does your staff *ever* get frustrated when it's time to use a monitor, and it hasn't been charging for very long, so they can't use it? Or they're even fighting over monitors?"

This happens all the time in real life.

Integration to charting system	"Does your staff *ever* complain that it's hard to remember the vitals? So they end up writing them on a little piece of paper and sticking in their pocket to chart later?"

This also happens all the time in real life.

Weighs only 3.5 pounds	"Has anyone *ever* mentioned that they would like a lighter monitor to carry around?"

They might keep them mounted on a wheeled pole, so this might not matter to them.

Proprietary blood pressure algorithm that has been known to be more comfortable than some of the competitors	"Do patients *ever* complain that the cuff is uncomfortable or too tight?"

Uncovering Pain Points Using the Magic Wedge Question

You might notice something all these wedge questions have in common. They're soft. Non-threatening. Remember the disarming we've worked so hard to do leading up to this? Keep it going.

The word "ever" is a great disarming word. It opens it up to any possible time this might have been a concern. Even if it's only once or twice, they might still mention it, as long as you're using the word "ever." They aren't going to serve up their secrets on a silver platter. We have to work for them.

When I do a seminar, we go through this as a big group. I ask people to shout out their unique competitive advantages, and inevitably, people begin by shouting out things you might read on a white paper, instead of really drilling down to true pain points. They will shout things like:

- Free training (This isn't a true advantage, because other vendors offer it too.)
- Integration to computer system (Others can do this as well, with a different technology, so it *could* be an advantage, but we need to dig deeper to figure out what's really going on and how ours is truly advantageous compared to others.)
- Award-winning customer support (Too vague.)

Let's pretend I'm doing a seminar, and we went deeper, and the sales reps identified a truly unique competitive advantage: A system they call EDGE, that is great for quicker test result processing. Let's pretend they shared with me that it is quicker than the competition, which customers love. Great. We're getting somewhere.

Now, many sales reps would suggest a wedge question like, **"Would it ever be helpful to process test results more quickly?"** This wedge question is... okay.

Of *course* they're going to think processing test results quicker would be cool. But that alone isn't their big headache, and that alone probably won't make them realize they need to spend money on your product. Dig deeper.

Ask yourself: what happens when they have to wait too long? Do doctors get mad? Do patients get sub-par care because meds get administered before the diagnosis is delivered? Does it cause other bottlenecks, creating a financial impact?

Once you answer *these* questions, and really put yourself in the customer's shoes, and into their daily life, you can start crafting some really strong wedge questions. Instead of that first wedge question, which was a little weak, consider these wedge questions instead:

- Do you ever run into issues where test results take so long to process that doctors get angry?
- Do patients ever get frustrated when they have to change meds because the results finally came back with an unexpected diagnosis?
- Does administration ever get upset when results take so long to process that it causes machines to sit empty?

With these questions, you're wedging in there, causing them to really think about pain points. This is how great conversations start, and how great salespeople uncover exactly what they will need to move to step three: framing up your solution. These better wedge questions give customers real-life examples that they can sink their teeth into, *and* they make your solution shine when it's time to get into that.

It's important to realize that sometimes well-meaning engineers and Research and Development folks assume they know what's important to customers, but it turns out they don't. Not always, anyway. We have to get to the bottom of what *really* matters to them

Uncovering Pain Points Using the Magic Wedge Question

to create this list, and the most important thing to remember is that each of these advantages has to be *solving a problem they have*, or *identifying a headache they might have or already have*, with their competitor's solution.

Once you write strong wedge questions, you will use them time and again, and you will start to understand *when* you should use each question. To become a master at this, you'll need to understand your competitors and fully understand their weak spots.

Spend some time putting together a spreadsheet, with specs and information on each competitor, including yourself. Only then can you make sure you're using the wedge questions to their full potential. That's how you set landmines for competitors and create a strategy for your own weak points.

This is essential to winning deals. Decent sales reps get basic, vague information about what customers want and need. Exceptional sales reps get detailed, rich information about pain points. And honestly, then you'll get to avoid headaches too! You'll have less objections to overcome at the end, less issues with pricing, and less competition to win the deal.

The worksheet located in Appendix D will help you craft your amazing wedge questions.

Qualifying Questions

We recently went through a car-buying process with my teenager. We entered the first dealership, and a lady asked us if we'd been helped. I said we hadn't, but just wanted to look inside a Kia Telluride quickly, because I was considering upgrading myself and giving my daughter my minivan.

She declined, asking me to come inside. I told her that I didn't want to waste her time if it was too small, so could she please just unlock it for us and if we were interested, we could move forward?

She declined again, forcing us to go inside. She asked us to sit down, explaining that before we could look inside a vehicle, she needed some basic information.

First, she asked my name, then for my address and phone number. She asked if Katie was my real name, or just a nickname and if I could please spell my full name. At this point, I'd had enough, and we left. Why she needed my full, legal name in order for me to peek inside the car, I'll never know.

At the next dealership, the guy kindly opened the car for us, and once we were interested, he **then** asked us to come inside. At that point, I was more than happy to share my information with him.

Your customer is just like me. They won't be dying to share all their basic information, such as decision-makers, budget, and timeline, **until** they're sure they're interested in your solution. Once they are, they will be more willing to give you all the information you need.

So, at some point during your discussion, you'll notice your customer getting antsy to finish the meeting. At that point, it's time to move the meeting into the final phase. You have two goals here:

1. Ask to frame up your solution either right now, or at a future meeting.
2. Get permission to ask a few qualifying questions.

You can say something like:

"I know you're busy, so I don't want to keep you any longer. Based on what you're telling me, I **do** think we have some solutions that will be really helpful for you. Would it make sense for me to come back, and I can bring the device and

Uncovering Pain Points Using the Magic Wedge Question

show you exactly how it might be able to help? Or should I show you a few things now?"

Let's say they agree to this. This means they're officially interested, so *now* is the time to frame up your solution. We will get into more specifics on how to do this in the next chapter, but for now, let's focus on the qualifying questions, which you'll bring up as the very last thing. You'll say, *"Just a few quick housekeeping things, if you don't mind? Will anyone else be involved in this process?"*

Do you see how I did this? I went right into it, but my question was disarming, so it worked. You might have been taught to ask questions like: *"What is your budget?"* or *"Who are the decision-makers?"* These are too direct. Too harsh. You need to soften your qualifying questions to get the answers you need before the customer gets defensive.

The following are some nice, soft ways to ask those pesky qualifying questions:

Avoid These	Instead Try
"Who are the Decision-Makers?"	1. "Will anyone else be involved in this process?" 2. "Is there anyone else who might have questions?"
"What is your budget?"	1. "Is this something you'll have to budget for?" (instead of asking what the budget actually is) 2. "Will you need delivery by a certain date?" 3. "Is there a deadline to submit your budget based on your fiscal year?"
"What is your timeline?"	1. "Will you want your equipment right away?" 2. "How does your timeline look for this? Do we have some time or will this be a bit of a rush?" (Do you see how soft that is? You're still getting what you need, but it's less threatening)
"What is your vendor selection process?"	1. "How does this process usually work?" 2. "Is there anything else I can do to help you get this request through your system?"

Softening your qualifying questions while also asking for clarification will give you the results you want. Now, you'll be able to enter data into the CRM for funnel-tracking purposes. After all, it's important to keep everyone on the inside happy too.

When You Hear "We're Just Not Interested"

No matter what you do, you're going to hear this occasionally. The customer might be in the middle of another important project, or perhaps they haven't budgeted for anything new. Worst case scenario, they have just purchased something similar and are happy with it.

This doesn't mean that all is lost and you should move on; it just means you have a longer sales cycle. This is a great way to start building a relationship. My favorite strategy if they tell you they're not interested is to use this phrase: *"Would it make sense for me to follow up in a few months to see if anything has changed?"*

It's non-threatening. Customers see it as a win, because they won't have to deal with you for a few months, and it's easier for them than telling you to get lost.

If they agree (which they do, about 99% of the time), you'll be able to call back and confidently say, *"Hi, this is Katie Mullen. When we chatted a few months ago, you asked me to follow up and see if anything has changed. Are you swamped?"* Be ready for them to tell you the same story. Polite persistence wins every time.

I had a customer tell me "not yet" every month for over two years. Eventually, I got the call. "Katie, we're finally ready to look at your stuff. It'll sure be nice to meet you in person after all these years."

By then, we'd built a really great relationship, and they felt they knew me well. That turned into one of the biggest deals I ever sold. Relationships take patience.

Chapter Summary

- Remember to disarm the customer. Never make them feel threatened.
- Think about your customer's day. You won't be able to come up with truly good wedge questions until you have thought through what their days look like.
- Save your qualifying questions for the end. They're not as important as gathering intel on pain points from the customer.
- Wait to present your solution until you know what the customer wants.

Uncovering Pain Points Using the Magic Wedge Question

Notes

7

THE SECRET TO GREAT MEETINGS AND PRESENTATIONS

I was twenty-five when I got my first sales job in medical equipment sales. It was an interesting setup because I was considered a "junior" sales rep, selling a lower-priced (and new-to-the-market) product, but the same customers I was selling to were also buying higher-priced products from more senior sales reps.

My senior sales rep got a call one day from our shared client. After years and years of a great partnership, with us being the sole vendor, they experienced some management changes, and had decided they wanted to consider other vendors. They invited us to participate in a bid process, referred to as an RFP, with our competitors.

Dagger to the heart.

I had been so excited to work with this customer, and now I might never have the chance if we couldn't win the bid. We began preparations. Our team consisted of several senior reps, me, and our manager.

We enlisted the help of our marketing team, and they gave us the recommended slides for this type of presentation. Apparently it was called a "dog and pony show" in the industry, and as a newbie, I wasn't really allowed to participate much (at all, actually) in the process.

I watched as our team put together a slide deck with eighty-seven slides. That seemed like a lot to me, and somewhere along the way, I began to suspect we were going about it all wrong. To me, it seemed a little... well, boring. But I'd been in sales for about two weeks at that point, and I was just a twenty-five-year-old kid. What did I know?

When the big day arrived, we were all nervous. The stakes were high, and we all knew it. Each sales rep sold different products to this customer, and they were all part of the larger contract, so if one of us lost, we all lost.

It took us five minutes to introduce ourselves. I began to sweat as I looked around the room. The audience was looking bored already. I began to wonder... did they really need to know the name and title of every person we had there? Were they going to be tested over this information?

We transitioned into the next part of our presentation, and we showed a photo of our company headquarters with some statistics about how many people we employed and our Fortune 500 ranking. The customers were now looking more bored and frustrated than ever. Finally, we went back and showed our company history starting in the 1960s. We had an entire slide with a timeline devoted to how we had evolved since then. We even included the founders' names and *their* entire work history, and how the names and products had evolved and changed over the decades.

I was sitting to the side during this part of the presentation, and I've rarely been so uncomfortable in my life. I could see the customers glance at each other, rolling their eyes. A few even started whispering. Clearly this wasn't landing well.

The Secret to Great Meetings and Presentations

A few customers left before our presentation was even finished. As you can imagine, the feedback from that presentation was... not great. They thought we were arrogant. We were floored by this. The reality was that we were so nervous we could barely speak! Even the senior reps had so much riding on this deal that they weren't immune to an incredible amount of nerves. I thought back to when customers were entering the room and finding their seats, and we didn't want to seem pushy, so we just stayed in the background, talking last-minute strategy to each other. Perhaps that came off as arrogant.

Next, they told us that we talked about ourselves too much. They said, "We know you. We've been using you for fifteen years. We didn't need to know all about your company history and your founding fathers. We wish you had focused more on <u>us</u>."

I was crushed to hear all the negative feedback, but from that point forward, I remembered something. I never interacted with a customer without hearing that phrase echoing through my mind: *Focus on Us.*

Now, I always focus on the customers, and it hasn't failed me yet. The truth is, customers don't care about us, and this was confirmed when I started my research project. Customers don't care about our company history, our awards and accolades, or about our founders. I hope this phrase will now echo throughout your brain forever: *Focus on Us.*

How to Focus on Them: Presentations

Presentations and meetings are similar, but an effective strategy varies for each. In both, you still want to follow the same general outline you learned already. First you disarm, then you get them talking, and then and only then, do you present your solution.

For a presentation, in a perfect world, you will have already accomplished steps one and two, and you are fully aware of all their hot buttons and compelling events that are pushing them to even consider making this purchase.

Before you ever step foot in the presentation, be prepared. Know your products. Know what the customer wants. Confirm that you have spoken to every decision-maker (if possible), and uncover any red flags *before* the meeting.

There is nothing worse than stepping into a meeting, only to find out that the competitor has been chatting with someone internally and helped change the scope of the entire project. Most of the work is going to be done *before* you get to your presentation. Make sure you:

- Have a friendly greeter from your team standing at the door as people enter the room. It's easy to get wrapped up in mentally preparing, but as I saw at my big dog and pony show, unintentionally ignoring customers is considered "arrogant."
- Keep conversation to a minimum between sales reps.

- Check in if necessary. Every single team member (even management!) should always follow the protocol designated by the customer.
- Don't display brochures at the beginning. People will automatically pick them up and start flipping through them, and won't listen to your carefully curated presentation. Save them for the end if necessary.
- Don't forget the power of the pause. When you talk slowly and give everyone a moment to process the information, they will be more interactive, and this is a beautiful thing.
- Use lots of energy. Practice smiling while you speak. Use your hands. Make eye contact. A highly energetic presenter is much more entertaining than a monotone one.

Consider Starting With a Story as Your "Hook"

I know I've told you never to talk about yourself. The one exception to this is the beginning of a presentation. Consider telling a story as your "hook" to get them interested. Similar to cold calling on the phone, the first few minutes are crucial to a presentation. We ***must*** grab their attention.

Storytelling is a time-honored tradition for sales, and for good reason.

- **Stories help our brains make sense of the world.**
- **Stories make things easier to remember.** It's more effective to teach with a story than with presentation of data.
- **Storytelling evokes a strong neurological response.** Stories allow us to focus because of the cortisol that is produced during the tense moments in the story. Plus, the happy ending sends us dopamine, making us feel more optimistic and giving us emotional involvement.[1]

Here's an example of a story I would tell; it worked well for me when I sold medical equipment:

"I used to say I would never drive a minivan. When I was a teenager, my parents **both** drove minivans. So I was the unfortunate student driver with only **minivans** for options. I vowed I would never go back, even as an adult.

But... then I had a baby. I don't know about you, but I had no idea how heavy one little baby in a carseat can be! I used to lug that baby around, and try to open the backseat in the wind, while holding the carseat and trying not to let the door hit the car next to me.

I began to hate my car with a passion. The seats were up so high that I had to climb up there and get into all sorts of strange positions to get my little daughter buckled up. When a friend told me about how the van has doors that automatically slide open, I began to think **maybe**, just **maybe** I could consider driving a van. So, without telling my husband, I went to test drive one. And wow, I have to say, I almost cried when I realized how much easier my life would be with doors that automatically slide open and **can't** hit the car next to me. No more fighting the wind. No more sore back and shoulder. I went home and talked to my husband that night, and within days, I had traded in my small SUV for a shiny new minivan. I never looked back. My day to day life is so much better because of this *one* change.

And that's why I'm here today. To talk to you about how much easier *your* life could be with our device. During my meetings with you over the past few months, I have learned that your staff is frustrated with (fill in the blank). I'm going to show you today how our device could alleviate that frustration, and hopefully, just like me with my minivan, make your life so much easier."

This story worked. It had all the elements of a good story, as outlined by renowned story-telling expert Doug Stevenson.[2] I set the scene. I took them on a journey with me. I explained the obstacle (the difficulty of lugging around a carseat). I explained what I did to overcome the obstacle (bought the dang minivan!), and then I resolved the story by making my point. My point in this case was: I will make your life easier if you buy my stuff.

Customers loved this story. They could relate, and it got their attention right from the start. It was much better than introducing them to people they would likely never meet again, such as my boss who flew in from St. Louis.

The problem with telling stories like this, though, is that they're kind of scary. It has to be a truly relevant story, and one that they can relate to. In my case, many of the stakeholders were women, and I knew they would relate to my minivan story. If you can't find a story like this that fits for you and your audience, or your key customer is an impatient driver, consider telling a *customer* story instead. You can describe how one of your customers was struggling with frustrations, and you were able to come in and solve their problems.

If you aren't comfortable with that either, just get right into it. Make sure you skip the introductions (boring!) and the company history (even more boring!), and save those for the end if necessary. Simply thank them for having you, and get right to the meat and potatoes.

What's Next

Here's what I suggest doing after you tell your story.

<u>Step One: Summarize What You Know About Them</u>

"I've enjoyed meeting with Susie and Bob, and I've discovered that the reason you need new equipment is because you're having trouble with nurses getting frustrated when..."

Expand here and summarize exactly what they told you.

"Does that sound about right?"

Wait for nods and give them time to expand on this if needed.

"In addition, I discovered that..."

Now add a few more hot buttons that you learned along the way.

The Secret to Great Meetings and Presentations

<u>Step Two: Make Sure You're Not Missing Anything</u>

"Okay, other than what we've already discussed, am I missing anything else important?"

Give them time to respond if needed. Things may have come up since the last time you spoke to them.

<u>Step Three: Frame Up Your Solution</u>

"Based on your needs, I think we can help you, and I'd like to show you how. First..."

Now you can really get into your products. They are interested, because they think you might actually be able to help solve their headaches, so they will be very receptive to hearing specifics.

Framing up your solution does not mean talking about you and your company. You are illustrating how **your products** address **their needs**. It's like fitting a puzzle piece into the right spot. If you have an amazing feature, but you know the customer doesn't care about that part, don't mention it here. Why? Because customers don't care about you. This is not a time for you to brag about all the amazing advantages you have over the competition. Keep it specific to what the customer needs. This is how you keep their attention.

And speaking of keeping their attention, if you need PowerPoint slides to frame up your solution, keep them simple. People tend to forget that there is a difference between *training* slides and *presentation* slides. With training slides, you need them to know lots of detail. That's actually the point of training people: you get into the weeds so they feel comfortable using the product by themselves. With **presentation** slides, they don't need to know everything. You want to give them enough information to help them make a decision and keep them interested, but boring them is a bad idea. And PowerPoint slides with small text are boring. Excruciatingly boring.

The problem with presentations is that the marketing team often wants to call the shots. They have prepared a slide deck full of the wrong kind of slides (sorry marketing teams, but it's true!). You will need to be your own advocate here, so you can avoid the mistakes that we made when we presented to our big customer early in my career. No matter what your marketing or management team says, no one wants to hear five slides worth of your company history. Trust me. And trust the customers I interviewed. They know what they want, and it's not that.

Step Four: Questions and Answers

Always be open to answering questions during any of the steps above. If the customer is engaged, they will likely have lots of questions as you start getting into the product discussions, but if not, make sure you leave plenty of time at the end. At this point, you may get a question about your company and what makes you qualified. Because of this, you should always have that slide about your company and who you are ready (and hidden) at the end of your presentation. If, and that's a big *if,* anyone cares, you will be fully prepared to talk about who you are. You might run across a customer from time to time who does want the comfort of knowing they're dealing with a legitimate and qualified business, but I bet it won't happen very often.

How to Focus on Them: Meetings

Meetings can be different from presentations. In a meeting, you might not have much information yet, so you'll need to spend time asking wedge questions.

Before I get into the nitty gritty of what a *good* meeting looks like, keep in mind a few other tips I heard from customers during my research that might help.

Have you ever been in a doctor's office and they're asking you questions about how you're feeling while looking down at their computer or iPad the entire time? It feels like they aren't listening, and it's very frustrating. Customers don't like this either.

Always remember:

- Come in with a good, old-fashioned pad of paper and a pen, and take notes on everything the customer is saying (not on an iPad!).
- If you give an ROI (Return on Investment), it must be accurate. Outlandish and unresearched ROIs make you look silly and discredit everything you're saying.
- Everyone has things we do and say that are annoying. Some people say, "Um" too much. Some say, "Ok?" after every sentence. Video yourself. Ask your colleagues to give you feedback, and have thick skin so you can get better. Your goal is to just not be annoying. Don't chew gum, don't be a close talker, don't have coffee breath, don't tell everyone your dreams.

You might be wondering why you need to hear these things. My research revealed that many, many sales reps still make these mistakes on a daily basis. You will rise above the rest if you ***don't*** do these things.

Now, on to what you should do. In a meeting, you'd likely want to skip the storytelling. A good meeting would look something like this:

Step One: Summarize What You Know So Far

First, always thank them, and confirm how much time you have. Next, summarize everything you know about them. Get into what you have learned from other stakeholders, and if you had a phone conversation with them ahead of time, remind them what you discussed and what you uncovered so far.

"Thanks so much for chatting with me on the phone last week. It sounds like your staff is having some frustration with the time it takes to get slides back from the lab. Does that sound right?"

This is the disarming portion of the meeting. Notice that you're not demanding to know when they will be buying the product and asking them if they are going to be the main decision-maker. This will put them on the defensive.

Let them talk. Hopefully you can open up a great discussion about why this specific topic is an issue for them, and you can be a great listener and get lots of rich detail that will help you when it's time to give your actual presentation. Silence works well here, and remember never to interrupt the customer, even if you're excited to show them how your product will help them.

Step Two: Ask Your Wedge Questions

The customer will need some help from you. They generally know why they're frustrated or at least interested in new equipment, but they need you to help them vocalize and identify all their concerns (If they could do this without you, salespeople wouldn't be nearly as valuable!).

That's where the wedge questions help. Because you're a

product expert, **and** you've spent time thinking through potential frustrations, you should have a great list of wedge questions you can ask to get the ball rolling. Once you hit a hot button, **be interested** and coax the information out of them by asking follow-up questions and waiting while they ponder their reply.

If they don't show an interest in a topic broached by your wedge question, move on. Resist the urge to be that guy and say, "Why don't you let me tell you about this anyway, just in case, because we're the only ones on the market with this cutting-edge technology."

Step Three: Ask for Permission to Briefly Frame Up Your Solution

Now you know exactly what matters to the customer, so you know what part of your solution is going to be a home run. It's finally time to frame up your solution:

> "Thank you so much. I loved learning about your team and your needs. Based on what you've shared, it does sound like we should be able to help you. Do you have time for me to go through a few things with you? Or will there be a presentation at some point?"

Let the customer guide you on how to proceed. Depending on their personality style, they may want all the excruciating detail you can provide about your product so they can determine if they're going to fight for you and your solution. On the other hand, they might think they have enough information to at least put you through to the next step.

Either way, make sure you determine next steps. Do you need to talk to someone else to move forward? Will there be a presentation with additional personnel? This would also be a great time to get answers to those qualifying questions you need, such as decision-makers, budget, etc. They are disarmed, warmed up, and probably ready to give you some additional information.

Never leave this meeting without getting one of three things: an introduction to a decision-maker, an invitation to present to a specific committee, or approval to send a quote.

Virtual Presentations Done Right

One of my favorite memories during my days as a sales rep is when we played Bingo. This wasn't your Grandma's Bingo. We created our own boards and came up with annoying phrases that people tended to say, and once we heard one, we could cross off that box.

This was especially fun during conference calls and virtual presentations. We used phrases such as:

- "Sorry, I was on mute."
- "Okay, are you seeing my screen?"
- "I'm sorry, someone just came to my door."

Once COVID-19 hit, virtual meetings and presentations became more common than ever, and we all know the pain of sitting through them: it's almost excruciating at times. The truth is, you should always choose an in-person meeting or presentation if you can. It's easier to read the room and adjust things according to body language. Also, it's much harder for your audience to ignore you and secretly check email during an in-person meeting.

However, sometimes it can't be avoided. When virtual meetings and presentations are necessary, there *are* some ways to make them more effective.

Preparation Is Key

Think through every detail. Make sure you have spoken to your customer ahead of time about who is attending and what to expect from their end, since you won't be able to see them in person.

Think through the flow. If you have multiple presenters from your side, make sure to designate a team leader. In the same way you would do it in person, have a "greeter" and a point person to decide when the meeting should officially start. Also, as you prepare your virtual presentation, minimize busy PowerPoints. This is more important than ever, and will allow people to focus more on what you're saying rather than trying to read your PowerPoint from their screen.

Think through how you will begin your virtual meeting. Will you thank them for coming? Will you introduce every team member? (Please don't!) If you're doing a full presentation, consider leaving out your "hook." It will fall a little flatter when you're not in person. People expect you to get to the heart of the matter more quickly in this format. A customer story might work better here if you have enough time.

The Technology

At the beginning, allow all attendees to join, and begin in full screen. Allow some conversation while you wait for all attendees, and this is where you will do your hook (if applicable) and summarize everything you know. You will mention why you're there, what you learned about their frustrations, and you will ask if anything has changed.

Do you have an extra computer? Use it. Sign in to the meeting as a ***guest*** on your extra computer. Set it up right next to your work computer, and you can glance at it anytime you're unsure what attendees can see. It will show you exactly what your customers are seeing. This will prevent you from presenting for fifteen minutes, thinking people are seeing your beautiful chart, only to realize later that no one saw it. Plus, this will allow you to *not* be the annoying person asking, "Can you see my screen?"

It's important to not only have an extra computer, but an extra monitor as well. If you're the type of person who takes notes on your PowerPoints, and you need to see these notes, having an extra monitor is the only way to do this. You will put your presentation in Presenter mode, and one screen will be what the rest of the attendees are seeing, and the other screen will show your slides.

In a virtual presentation, eye contact is really difficult. Your tendency will be to look at customers in the eye, as you would in person, but this doesn't land well because you don't appear to be making good eye contact. Your personal connection to the customer will suffer. It almost seems like you're looking down when you do this. Instead, you want to look at the ***camera, not the screen*** (the camera is usually the dot at the top of your screen) while *you* are speaking. This nuance is what makes the participants feel you are actually looking them in the eye, and is why virtual presentations are so tricky, so practice is key.

While *they* are speaking, feel free to look around at the other attendees on the screen so you can read body language. Eye contact isn't as important here for you, since they are the ones speaking.

If someone interrupts and starts asking questions, which leads to a discussion, switch back to full screen. Once the discussion is finished and you're ready to continue with your presentation, you can start sharing your screen again.

Resist the urge to start sharing your slides too early. Allow for discussion, while in full screen. Only when everyone agrees that you have all the facts will you switch over to your presentation if needed.

Consider investing in a mobile desk. I bought one a few years ago that moves up and down, and it's been a life-changer. Now I don't have to stack books on my desk to make sure my screen is at the correct angle.

The most flattering and effective angle for your computer monitor is for it to be slightly above you, rather than slightly below you. Play around with it, and see what looks best. Avoiding virtual presentations isn't a reality in today's world, so we must learn to embrace them and do them well.

Chapter Summary

Always remember to keep the focus on the customer, and not on your company's history and product portfolio.

- Avoid all customer pet peeves. Make sure you take the time to find out everything you can and speak to every decision-maker ahead of time.
- Always frame up your solution around one of their frustrations/problems. Never present a feature just for the sake of it.
- For virtual presentations, focus on eye contact, minimize busy PowerPoints, and encourage discussion and interaction as much as possible.

The Secret to Great Meetings and Presentations

<u>Notes</u>

SECTION III

NEW WAYS TO SELL: TOOLS YOU MIGHT NOT THINK YOU NEED

8

SOCIAL SELLING: WHY LINKEDIN IS YOUR NEXT BEST FRIEND

My son loves to fish. In the summers, he doesn't even mind waking up super early at the lake house, so he can get out on the water in time to "catch the good fish."

When he was about ten, he decided that fishing with worms wasn't good enough. He had started watching YouTube videos of bass fishermen, and became convinced he needed more technology. Since this hobby is much better than him being stuck on screens all day, I immediately agreed to take him to Bass Pro Shops®.

I was both horrified and amazed at the sheer volume of options for lures, bait, and poles. Luckily, a nice man named Bob was kind enough to spend over an hour with us, educating us on all the options. My son and I were mesmerized and walked away with a bag full of lures, $150 poorer, and feeling like we still had a lot to learn about fishing.

As we pulled out of the parking lot, it occurred to me that fishing is not a new thing. Even back in biblical times, they somehow figured it out, without handy salesmen like Bob. They didn't even use poles. They just threw nets into the ocean, instead of using fancy tools like smuggle lures and GPS-enabled bobbers.[1] And it worked.

Just like fishing, sales is not a new career. People have been selling things for thousands of years. The question is: can you be a proficient salesperson without fancy new tools like LinkedIn? Yes.

Does that mean you should?

I would say... no! My son *could* swear off modern tools and just throw his net off the dock, but that doesn't mean he *should*. Times have changed, and so must we.

At the least, you should educate yourself on LinkedIn so you can decide if it's worth your time. It can create opportunities for you, and not just new career opportunities. It can also give you the ability to find customers, learn about them and their buying habits, and even gather new leads.

Hopefully by now you realize how important it is to become not only a farmer, but also a hunter. Discovering untapped markets is the only way to make sure you have a healthy funnel at all times. A wise friend used to tell me that I need to have at least twice, if not three times, my quota in my funnel at all times.

Let's say that your quota is $1,000,000. This means you need to have $2,000,000 in your funnel, if not $3,000,000. Why? Because not every deal works out. Some deals go to the competitor. Some get pushed back to another calendar year. Things happen, and that's why you need so much extra cushioning.

You can create extra cushioning by becoming a new kind of salesperson: a magnet.

Becoming a magnet is like opening your front door to go for a walk, and on your porch you find a nicely wrapped gift you weren't expecting. You didn't have to do anything for it. It just appeared, simply because you're such a great person.

When you use LinkedIn effectively, leads appear on your doorstep. You don't have to seek them out, or call them eight times before you get a response. Forget hunters and farmers. Become a magnet.

Appealing to the Right Audience

Most people in sales are proud of their accomplishments. We love to outline our percent-to-quota attainment on LinkedIn. We love to tell the world when we win the Pinnacle Award for top sales rep.

Customers, on the other hand, do *not* love to read about these accomplishments. In fact, it's irritating to them. They don't get lovely trips to Puerto Rico. They might only get donuts in the break room, so we need to be mindful of what we put on our LinkedIn profiles.

The question is: are you looking for a new job? Or new customers?

If you're actually looking for a new job, feel free to post about all your accomplishments in their glory. Recruiters will love to hear about it, and that should help you land your next great sales role. However, if you're happy with your current position, and want to get new leads or connect with customers on LinkedIn, it's time to erase all that sales data.

Make sure to save it in a file somewhere, so you can pull it back out and use it when it's time to start job-hunting again. But for now, we need to appeal to the customer by highlighting how helpful you are to customers, and not how rich you're becoming as a sales rep.

6 Key Aspects for a Strong *Customer-Facing* Profile

1. Maximize Your Connections

500 (yes, you read that right: 500) connections is your goal, but you can probably do even better than that, unless you're just starting out in the business world. The algorithm will suggest potential connections from your contacts, but you can also search for specific people. Think through old friends, neighbors, family friends, former colleagues, and customers.

The more people you are connected with, the more people will see your posts. If an old neighbor likes your post, people in his network will see your post, and possibly either react to your post, start following you, or request a connection. This is your ideal scenario. Spend several hours thinking through all potential connections, and then make a commitment that moving forward, you will make an effort to connect with **all** customers and colleagues.

When you do reach out to customers, it's better to wait until you've had some interaction with them, rather than reaching out before you have even started prospecting. They aren't as likely to accept your connection request until you're a familiar name.

When you do reach out, I have discovered some language that really maximizes the chances they will accept your request:

> "Hi Jeff, I'm your XYZ Company Rep, and I would be honored to be in your network. Hope you have a great weekend!"

There is something about this language that really works. People love the complimentary, but sincere, language.

The key is to make sure you never try to sell them something on LinkedIn, and don't bother with InMail messages. In my opinion, they don't tend to work. (Sorry, LinkedIn!) Instead, focus on maximizing your number of connections and posting content that provides *value*. I have followed up with many of the reps I have taught over the years, and on average, the people who embrace this strategy are getting a handful of leads every week. It really does work.

2. A Great Job Description

This is the one area where you can brag a little about your company. Keep it minimal, but feel free to state how long you've been around, and what you can offer. Outline exactly what you're selling and what territory you cover. This way, if a customer finds you and your profile, they will be able to quickly assess whether you're the person they should be talking to for their desired products and area of the country.

The following is an example of a former client. Focusing on great job descriptions has worked well for him for the past several years.

> *Associated Imaging Services was started in 1990, and our #1 priority is customer service. We are proud to be a reliable and affordable resource to clinics and hospitals throughout our area.*
>
> *AIS provides a wide variety of products, including:*
>
> - *New Mindray Diagnostic Ultrasound*
> - *Refurbished Ultrasound Equipment manufactured by various vendors including GE, Philips, Siemens, Toshiba, Medison, and more*

- *New Mediso Nuclear Medicine Cameras*
- *Refurbished Nuclear Medicine Cameras manufactured by various vendors, including GE, Siemens, ADAC (Philips), SMV, and more*
- *Phone tech support*
- *Experienced and knowledgeable service engineers*

3. A Strong Summary Section

This section should be written in first person, and should be warm and easy to understand. The customer should feel like they're talking directly to you. This isn't easy to do, and if you think you can't focus on this, it's better to leave it blank than fill it up with your sales achievements.

If you do choose to spend some time on it, you can make it great by writing in third grade level, just like we did for writing emails. Keep it simple, conversational, and relatable. Show your dedication to your customers, and keep it short and sweet. Feel free to mention your company, and what makes your products great, but minimize marketing language.

Grant Norris has a great summary on LinkedIn that has worked well for him (and I helped him write it, so I'm a little biased, but he has had great luck with it):

My greatest skill as a salesperson is my ability to listen to my customers because I have learned that every customer is different. What works for one may not work for another so I make sure to ask lots of questions and try to understand the day to day life of my customer so that I can try to come up with the best possible solution for their needs. It might be a cutting-edge ultrasound system or a nuclear medicine camera, or it might even be to provide service for another vendor's product. Whatever the case may be, I give my full attention to each customer, and my customers appreciate my attention to detail and my passion for making their lives easier.

This passion for listening emphatically began when I was a teacher. I spent almost seven years as a high school teacher and baseball coach, and during that time I enjoyed meeting and interacting with a variety of people and personalities. While I loved my time in the field of education, I felt drawn to the medical field and decided to make the switch in 2004. I truly enjoy every day I spend meeting with customers and helping them meet their clinical and servicing needs.

On a side note, you can do this same thing if you are actually looking for a job. You would still write in first person, and keep the language relatable, but keep the focus on your sales skills, rather than the customer. Here is an example of one that I wrote for an old client. After posting this, he heard from a recruiter almost right away, and he landed his first job in medical equipment sales. He went on to get an even better job shortly after with a Fortune 500 company in the medical device world.

I am good at sales for two reasons: I am competitive, and I learned at a young age that if you take care of the little things, the big things will take care of themselves.

I was born with a competitive nature and this began to show when I started playing sports in grade school, high school, and then on to college. I discovered that I thrive and my teammates thrive when I take a leadership role. I played shortstop in baseball, making sure my teammates knew where to go during every situation. I played safety and quarterback in football, also making sure my teammates knew what was going on around them. I learned how to be a leader, and I transfer those skills every day to my sales career.

Perhaps even more important than my competitive nature is my ability to connect with my customers. I show my customers that they are incredibly important to me. It could be as simple as saying thank you for the business, or sending a thank-you card after a meeting, but whatever it is, my customers know that I value them.

My customers know that I value them, and I have a strong desire to succeed. This combination is what has made me successful so far, and what will continue to make me successful in the future.

4. Recommendations Section

Never be afraid to call a customer and ask for a referral for the recommendations section on LinkedIn. My research shows that most customers are happy to write one for good vendors, but hardly any sales reps actually ask.

To make it easier on them, they might ask you to write it up yourself, and send it to them so they can copy and paste it. Jump on this opportunity. They can always tweak it later. These recommendations will also come in handy if and when you start a new job search, so make this a priority. Make it your goal to have at least three recommendations from customers on your profile.

5. A Professional (and Strong) Photo

Don't take a photo from your dad's latest birthday celebration and crop out your brother. I've seen this too many times: you can still see his hand, no matter how well you crop it. It's not professional.

Spend the money to have a real headshot taken. It's not as expensive as you might think, and most of the time, you can probably expense it. Oh, and don't take a photo from fifteen years ago and throw it up there. You have aged. Roll with it.

You also want to make sure you look friendly and warm in your photo. If you think you might have heard that before, you're right! Make sure to smile, and get feedback from your friends and co-workers on how you truly look.

I had a friend once, who was a super nice guy, but his profile picture was super creepy. I finally told him. It was a bit of an awkward conversation, but he appreciated me telling him because he didn't realize it. So it's important to get opinions from others, since it's the first impression you might have on a customer.

If you do all these little things, you'll have a profile that will make customers think you're professional, approachable, and someone they want to work with. Even if you can do some of this, you'll be making good progress and likely be better than 80% of your competitors. If you want to get a feel for how you're doing, check out the self-evaluation worksheet in Appendix E.

6. Understand the Algorithm

Now that you understand how to have a solid profile, it's important for you to learn the LinkedIn algorithm. LinkedIn is a news feed, which is different from YouTube. On YouTube, someone might seek out answers to specific problems. For example, let's say your dog has an accident on your new white rug. You'll head to YouTube and search for ways to clean it.

With LinkedIn, no one is seeking anything except... entertainment. At the end of the day, LinkedIn is a way for people to be entertained and also make important business connections. People scroll, not sure what they'll find, and this is why it's your job to provide *unique* value, or entertainment.

The good news is that the algorithm favors new content creators. If you've never posted before, and you suddenly start posting, you'll get tons of views. Plus, do you know what percentage of people actually post? When I do a seminar, most people guess the number to be around 10-20%.

The answer is less than 1%.[2] This means you have a huge amount of opportunity, especially if you're posting the right things.

So, how can you make sure your content gets seen?

- Connect with as many people as possible.
- Post something of *value*.
- Be mindful of the algorithm. Never anger it.

The LinkedIn algorithm is always testing you. How well your post performs in the first hour is crucial. If you can, text a friend or two (or ten) and let them know you just posted, and ask them to comment. This will ensure that it gets pushed out to more of your network (and those first and second degree connections outside your network).

You can also maximize your visibility by using hashtags. You can test hashtags by going to the search bar and typing in the hashtag you are considering. After you type a few letters, it will pop up as an option. Click on it, and you will be able to see how many people follow that particular hashtag. For example, at this point in my career, I try to appeal to sales reps, so when I use the sales hashtag, I maximize my potential because over five million people follow this hashtag.

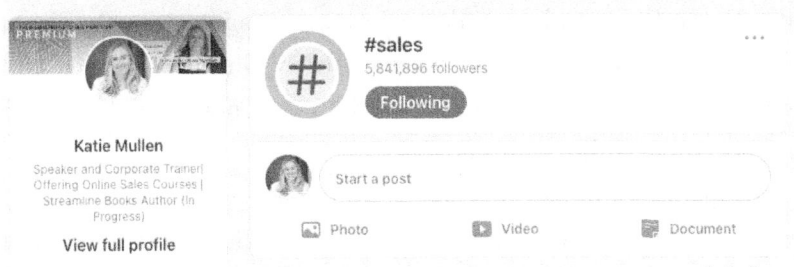

In contrast, sales coaching may seem like a good hashtag, but it's not:

Play around a little, and come up with a handful of hashtags you can use in your posts that will be beneficial for you in your industry. Feel free to use them over and over again.

Posting Value

With LinkedIn, the most important thing to remember is that you must post something of value. Many people are confused about what that means. This might help: if you start your post with something like, "We're proud to announce…" you know you have failed. This isn't providing value, it's bragging.

People often try to start posting on LinkedIn by re-posting their company's content, which usually links to an article on the company website. This doesn't work for two reasons. First, people skip commercials. If you post a commercial, which is what this is, no one cares. Second, from my experience, the LinkedIn algorithm doesn't like you to steer people *away* from LinkedIn, so they will penalize you for this, suppress your post, and not show it to many of the people within your network.

A great example of this is a post I did a few years ago, where I wrote a story and linked it (incorrectly) in the body of the post, and it performed terribly: only five likes and thirty-seven views. I decided to experiment, and a few months later, I posted the exact same article, but this time, I put all the words in the body of the post, and didn't link to anything. It was literally the exact same information, just in a different format. It garnered 27,407 views, 321 likes, and 119 comments. A stunning difference. I have dozens of examples of sales reps making this small change, and they tend to go from just a few likes to dozens or more.

The lesson I learned? ***Post words, not articles.***

You might be able to get around this algorithm issue by summarizing the information in your company's article in your own words, and then linking the article in your comments. This is better than posting nothing, but you can do better. Dig deeper, and get more creative. Provide something people actually care about.

You can do this by:

- Offering valuable information
- Offering free training/webinars
- Telling an interesting story (most likely personal)

Here is an example of how your company can offer a free webinar in a way that makes it interesting to your network:

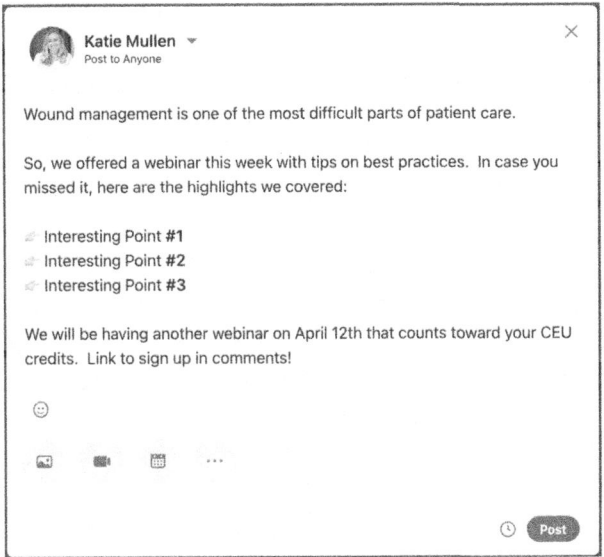

Or, here is another idea:

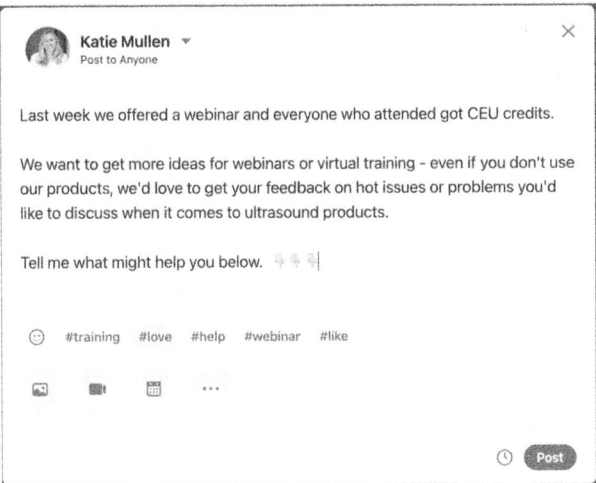

Telling a personal story is also a great way to go. Try something like this:

I have even seen people have success posting photos of their team at a sales event. It's interesting. It's relatable.

Another great option would be to post a story about an installation that went well. You'd have to get your customer's permission, but if you can, and your company allows this, it tends to create the highest amount of leads. Customers see first-hand that other people are buying from you, it's going well, and you're a responsible and attentive sales rep. And that's a win for everyone.

Here is an example of this. A former client posted this on LinkedIn, and look at those views and likes. This is an outstanding amount of interaction from someone with less than 1,000 connections.

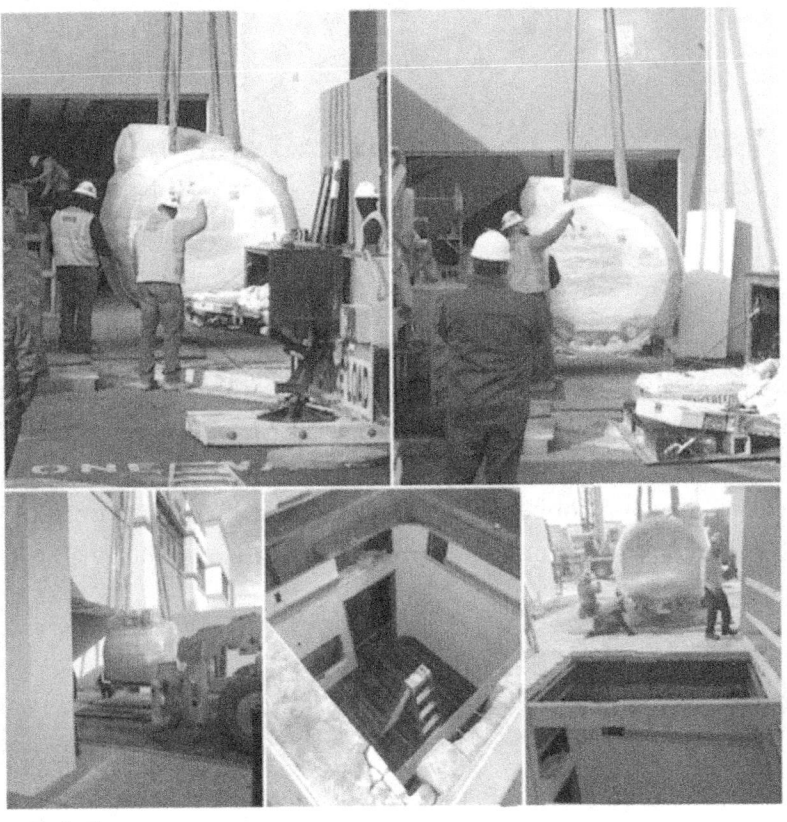

This post worked because it was interesting, and it didn't take anyone *away* from LinkedIn. Compare that to the post shown in the next image. In this, the same person simply re-posted a company article. Hardly any interaction at all. Same person, same number of connections, different content. Big difference. Huge.

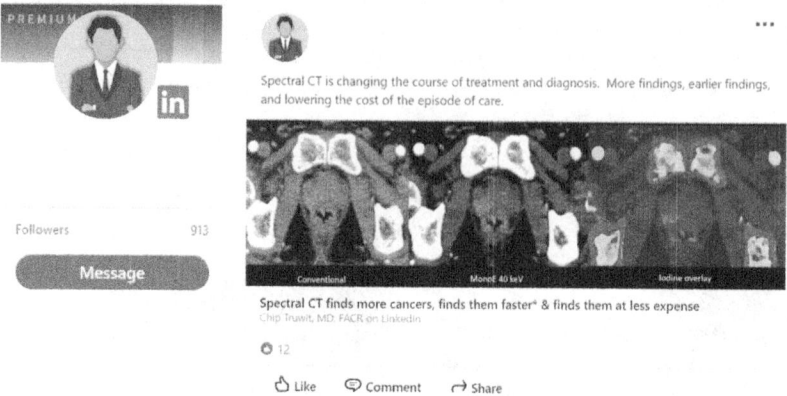

LinkedIn is often an unfamiliar and sometimes intimidating tool, but we might as well embrace it. It's here for you. Choose to be the rep that takes this and runs with it. Some people might think having a fishing bobber with GPS-enabled technology to track fish is cheating, but it's not, and using LinkedIn isn't either. It's what smart sales reps do.

Chapter Summary

- Remember to write your profile for your intended audience. Is that customers or recruiters? You decide.
- Write a great profile that includes a lot of connections, a well-written summary, detailed job descriptions, and several customer recommendations.
- When you post, provide something of value. Don't rely on your company to give you an interesting post. Get creative.
- Never post a link to an article. Always link to articles in your comments if necessary.

Notes

9

VIDEO MESSAGING: THE SECRET WEAPON OF SALES

I run my own company, and that can be a little scary. In fact, I will admit that when I first started out, it was *really* scary. I knew I had a lot to offer, and I knew I had developed a training curriculum that could really help sales teams, but it just so happened that many of my target customers were Fortune 500 companies.

Would they really take me seriously?

Then one day, I had a call scheduled with a **Fortune 100** company. Yikes. Little old me, who works alone and spends a lot of time in my backyard and playing driveway basketball with my kids.

How would it go?

Actually, it went pretty great, and here's why: I utilized a tool called video messaging. You might be thinking this sounds like a lot of work, and you might be wondering if this is really going to be worth the trouble.

It is. You see, I had developed a rapport with a lower-level manager at this Fortune 100 company, and he was interested in hiring me for his sales team. He was willing to go to bat for me and introduce me to his managers and the HR manager, but that worried me because I had been burned before.

"Why don't you send me a proposal?" he said. "Include a brochure, and I'll take it to my boss and see if she's interested."

I had been down this road many times before. Usually, once you send the email, it's crickets. You wait and wait and follow up and... nothing.

But this time, I had a secret weapon. I put together the brochures and information as requested, but this time, I asked for the name of the manager, and I made her a short video. The script went something like this:

"Hi Suzanne, I've really enjoyed getting to know Mark, and he filled me in on your situation. It sounds like you have several newer sales reps, and you've been talking a bit about doing some sales training at your meeting this summer. I would love to talk with you about what I can offer. I'm hoping perhaps we can set up a time to chat, maybe sometime next week? I included some additional info—let me know how next week looks for you. Thanks!"

You know what Suzanne said when she finally met me? "Katie, it's great to meet you! Although I feel like I already know you from your video!"

Video messaging is like sending a voicemail, but they *see you* as well, so it's warmer and more effective. My research shows that the majority of customers are open to receiving a video message, and it's not something that many sales reps do, so it allows you to stand out.

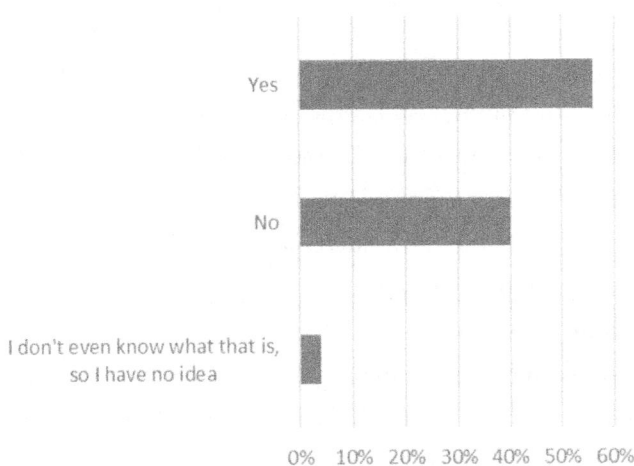

Customers receive so many emails that they end up deleting most of them every day. We spend so much time figuring out how to send an email that stands out, and video messaging is an amazing way to do this.

I taught this method in a seminar one time, and one of the sales reps embraced the strategy and went out and tried it right away. He sent a video message to a customer who had ghosted him for weeks. He didn't know why this was happening and was concerned because it was a faithful customer who usually responded.

After receiving the video message, the customer called almost immediately with a laughing, apologetic tone, and a plan was set for an in-person meeting later in the week. My sales rep was thrilled. He thought he had tried everything and was starting to feel like a pest and didn't know what else to do. The video message was the only thing that worked.

Here's when video messaging works well:

- **To accompany a pricing proposal.** When we send pricing, we often have to send a long email to explain exactly what we quoted and why. I don't know about you, but I often wish I could just get the person on the phone because it would be so much easier to explain in person, rather than via email. Plus, long emails are super annoying. The video message helps with this. You can explain as you would if you were in person with them.
- **To get in front of a manager.** Some sales experts say you should always sell top to bottom. I disagree. It really depends on the customer. Some of my biggest sales started with lower-level managers, and then we navigated to higher level decision-makers. Video messaging is a great way to do this. Get your lower-level contacts to agree to pass along your video message, and you'll be amazed at how it can open up doors for you.
- **As a second step after your initial meeting.** You can summarize how the meeting went, and what next steps will be.
- **As a strategy for when customers ignore you.** Just like my student who tried this, you will find this is a really effective strategy to get in touch with elusive customers.

Here's when video messaging does *not* work well:

- **When you've never talked to the person before.** The customer will be much less likely to look at or click on a video message if they've never spoken to you before. Save videos for established relationships.

- **When there is a delicate topic and you need to get something in writing to cover your bases.**
- **When your company is concerned about the legality of "making product claims."** I have occasionally seen companies that have strict rules about what sales reps can legally say about products. If you feel like you're in this boat, make sure you talk to your manager. Generally, if you can put it in an email, you can probably put it in a video message, but don't make claims about your product being better or more effective because that probably won't be legal and could get you in trouble.

Some sales reps are going to read this and decide to really embrace this new technology. Others will decide it's too scary or time-consuming. If you're one of the ones who decides to embrace it, it's important to remember that you should never, ever send a video as an attachment to an email. The message will be too large and will most likely get blocked from the customer's email servers, even if your server allows you to send it.

Here are the ways you can send the message instead:

- **As a text message** (especially if you know the customer fairly well and have texted them before).
- **As a LinkedIn private message.** Note that this only works if you're first degree connected to the customer. LinkedIn doesn't allow video messages for second and third degree connections.
- **Through email with a YouTube hyperlink.** The advantage of doing it this way is that it's free. I recommend setting up a new account, because if you're anything like me, you share your YouTube account with your kids, and as soon as the video is over, it will suggest

other videos from your YouTube history. If I were to use my normal YouTube, the customer would soon see riveting conspiracy theory videos on why Darth Vader isn't *really* Luke's dad, courtesy of my 13-year-old. Creating a new account keeps things nice and clean. You'll also want to take a screenshot of you talking, preferably smiling, and you will paste that into the body of the email, with a hyperlink to the video you created.

- **Through a third-party service, such as Vidyard, BombBomb, Loom, or my personal favorite, Sales Mail.** This is a great way to do video messaging, for a few reasons. It can be much faster than sending through YouTube. Plus, you can keep track of who has seen your message and get some great intel on when and where they're viewing from. The disadvantage is that sometimes the email servers block the images associated with these messages if you aren't a trusted sender. This is another reason to never bother with this method until you've established a relationship with the customer.

An ideal video message is less than sixty seconds. Thirty seconds is probably even better. The only exception would be if you were using it to explain a complicated pricing proposal and in that case, it's okay to make it a little longer.

Make sure you use good lighting. You can buy an inexpensive light from Amazon for less than $30, and it will make a big difference to your video experience. Then, set up an area in your house where you have the chair and the light easy to access for all your videos. If setup is minimal, you'll be much more likely to actually do the videos and stick with it.

And I recommend you *do* stick with it. Isn't it great to find ways to stand out in sales? Sometimes it seems like all the good stuff has already been tried. Not this. This is something you can do that's creative and different. Wouldn't it be great for a high-level decision-maker to say they feel like they already know you? It's worth your time to learn and implement this important skill.

Chapter Summary

- Set up an area of your house where you can easily and quickly make a customer video. Focus on good lighting and quick setup.
- Never send videos to customers you don't know, but use often for customers you do know, for pricing proposals and follow-ups.
- Use video messaging strategically to get to higher-level decision makers.

Video Messaging: The Secret Weapon of Sales

<u>Notes</u>

CONCLUSION: BRINGING IT ALL TOGETHER

Trent Dyrsmid was inexperienced when he first started as a stockbroker back in 1993, but he had a plan. Each morning, he showed up to work with two jars. One was empty. The other held 120 paper clips. Every time he made a sales call, he would move one paper clip. His goal was to move every paper clip each day, resulting in 120 sales calls.

In less than two years, he went from a rookie sales rep, with no revenue, to bringing in over $5,000,000 for his company. This story was introduced to me by James Clear, the author of *Atomic Habits*, and he shared it as an example of why tracking our habits is so powerful.

I loved this story for a different reason, though, because it reminded me of my first sales role. It was an inside sales job, where we worked in the office. They tracked every phone call, recorded them, and played them back for the group, critiquing us on what we could have done better.

It was completely nerve-wracking when they played our calls back for the group, but I wasn't nervous when they reported our *volume* of calls. I typically made between 100 to 150 calls per day. I was new. I didn't have anything better to do.

Some of my co-workers consistently didn't make more than *twenty* calls. This made me unpopular within our office, since I set the bar so high, but the results were clear. Making over 100 calls per day yielded results. I was bringing in clients faster than anyone in the office **because I was making the most calls, and doing it consistently.**

The last thing any sales rep wants is for their funnel to dry up, and it surely will if you don't put in the time, week after week. Sure, times have changed since I started in sales in 2002. Tools like LinkedIn and video messaging have made our lives easier, and made prospecting more effective. I highly recommend you use any tool at your disposal, but remember... we still have to pick up the phone and send prospect emails, and often. There's no getting around it.

And as you pick up the phone, always remember what the customer would say to you if they could: *Focus on us.*

We have to walk that fine line when we're in sales, but now you can ensure you won't get lost, because you know how customers think. You're equipped to treat them exactly the way **they** want to be treated and they will love you for it... I promise.

Thank you for taking this journey with me. I loved writing this book, and welcome you to reach out on LinkedIn and share your journey (and hopefully successes) with me. We're all in this together.

QR CODE: DIGITAL DOWNLOADS

To get a digital copy of this worksheet, visit www.thesalestightrope.com/book/worksheets or scan the QR code:

APPENDIX A

Mirroring Personality Styles Worksheet

NAME: _____   DATE: _____

Person	Name	Personality Type	How will you adjust your style to match their personality in a way you never have before?
You			
Your manager			
Peer #1			
Peer #2			
Peer #3			
Customer #1			
Customer #2			
Customer #3			
Customer #4			
Additional			
Additional			
Additional			
Additional			
Additional			

Directions:

1. Complete the personality quiz and enter your information above.
2. Identify your manager's likely style and reflect on how you can communicate and work better with your manager, based on his/her style
3. Do the same for several peers, customers, and anyone else that is helpful to you.

QR CODE: DIGITAL DOWNLOADS

To get a digital copy of this worksheet, visit
www.thesalestightrope.com/book/worksheets or scan the QR code:

APPENDIX B

Letter Worksheet

NAME: _____   DATE: _____

Build Your Letter	Examples	Your Letter
Friendly Greeting (Optional)	Happy New Year.	
	Happy Friday.	
Introduction sentence - Simply Introduce yourself, your company, and what you sell	I am the specialist for the new Thomas Medical vital signs monitor, and I wanted to reach out and introduce myself.	
Talk about them - research you've done or the fact that you're interested in learning more about them	I loved your post recently on the patient safety measures that your hospital has been taking. OR if they haven't posted anything and you can't find anything about them that is meaningful - I have heard great things about Methodist Hospital and would be excited to learn more about your facility and your department	
Introduce your product	The ASI is a brand-new roll around device for taking vital signs. Here are a few features that might interest you:	
Bullets	Any facts about your device or product, that you can pull from a brochure or fact-sheet	
Call to Action - When will you follow up?	I would love to schedule a time to meet to learn more about your needs. I will plan to follow up next week, but please feel free to reach out in the meantime.	
Closing	Kind regards, OR Best,	

Directions:

1. Take a close look at the examples.
2. Think through what works for you and enter your information into each box.
3. Look at the sample letter provided and use the information to create your own template letter.

QR CODE: DIGITAL DOWNLOADS

To get a digital copy of this worksheet, visit
www.thesalestightrope.com/book/worksheets or scan the QR code:

APPENDIX C

Call Script Worksheet

NAME: _____ DATE: _____

Build Your Script	Examples	Your Script
Basic Introduction	• Hi Kelly, this is Mike from MMS	
Opening line	• Silence after intro. • Are you swamped? • I wanted to follow up on the information I sent. Did you receive it okay? • Are you familiar with us at all? • I know this is a cold call and you're probably swamped. I'd love to take a few minutes to explain why I'm calling and then if you want, you can hang up (laugh) • This is a cold-call, so I understand if you want to hang up (laugh), but I'd love to introduce myself and see if IV Poles (insert your category here) are on your radar at all?	
In-Depth Introduction	• I wanted to reach out and introduce myself. I'm in charge of the new IV pole that has just come out. (Silence) • I wanted to reach out and introduce myself. I'm in charge of the new IV pole that has just come out. (and go right into the next part)	
Questioning 1	• What are you using for that now?	
Questioning 2	• Oh, I see. Are those pretty new? • Oh, great. Are those working out pretty well for you? • Good deal. How are those working out for you? (not ideal)	
Questioning 3	• Oh, I see. Are those pretty new? • Oh, great. Are those working out pretty well for you? • Good deal. How are those working out for you? (not ideal)	
If they say the devices are fairly old, move it forward in a non-threatening way using disarming words (underlined)	• Interesting. So it sounds like it might make sense to start looking to replace those down the line. Is that on your radar <u>at all?</u> • Have you <u>ever</u> thought about looking into replacement options?	
Invite them to share more	• Oh? • Interesting. Anything else • I'd love to hear more (okay, but not as good) • Tell me more (okay, but not as good)	
Wedge Questions	• Is battery life ever an issue? • Do your nurses ever complain about the rooms being too crowded with equipment? • Would it ever be helpful to have the information go directly into your charting system?	
Move it forward if it sounds like a good short-term opportunity	• It sure sounds like our new IV pole could be a good fit for you when you decide to replace those IV poles. • Would it make sense for us to meet?	
Move it forward if it doesn't sound like a good short-term opportunity	• It sounds like the timing isn't great right now, since you still have some fairly new equipment. <u>Would it make sense</u> for me to follow up in 3 or 6 months to see if anything has changed?	

Directions:

1. Take a close look at the examples
2. Enter your own preference for each of these. What makes sense for your products and your personality?
3. Now use the information you entered to create a call script that resembles the sample call script provided.

QR CODE: DIGITAL DOWNLOADS

To get a digital copy of this worksheet, visit
www.thesalestightrope.com/book/worksheets or scan the QR code:

APPENDIX D

Product Features and Wedge Questions Worksheet

NAME: DATE:

Sample Product Features	Wedge Question Examples	Disarming Words Used
8 Hours Battery Life	Is Battery Life Ever an Issue?	Ever
4 Hours Recharge Time	Would it make your staff happy if the recharge time was shorter? Or is that something they wouldn't care about?	Or is that something they wouldn't care about? (Reverse question. Makes them want to answer yes)
Integration to charting system	Would it ever be helpful to have the information go directly to your charting system?	Ever
3.5 pounds (lighter than competitors)	Has anyone ever mentioned that they would like a lighter monitor?	Ever
Proprietary blood pressure algorithm	Would patients appreciate a more comfortable cuff?	Would, appreciate

Your Product Features	Your Wedge Questions	Disarming Words Used

QR CODE: DIGITAL DOWNLOADS

To get a digital copy of this worksheet, visit
www.thesalestightrope.com/book/worksheets or scan the QR code:

APPENDIX E

LinkedIn Self Evaluation

NAME: DATE:

Criteria	Ideal Criteria	Your Profile	Meet Criteria?
Number of connections	500+		
Profile picture	Must have one and have scores of at least 7 on Photofeeler		
Number of Endorsements	At least 3 from customers		
Summary	Written in first person, geared toward meeting customer needs		
Job description	Written in 3rd person. Describes your territory, and your products so that someone could easily figure out if you are the correct sales rep		
Contact info	Must give customers a way to get in touch, and include your company website		
Personal info	None should be included, except perhaps some volunteer information, if applicable		
Activity commenting on your customer's posts	Are you commenting and liking if and when your customer posts something?		

ACKNOWLEDGMENTS

Thank you to my husband, Scott, for always believing in me and telling anyone who will listen that I'm much smarter than he is. I love that about you and I'm so happy we decided to do life together.

Next, thank you to my kids, Anna and Carter. Thank you for always asking about my work, and for giving me your opinions on my title and book cover. You are truly awesome kids and I'm so lucky to have you.

Thank you to my parents. You support our family through everything, from rabbit shows to moving houses to writing books. You are the best parents anyone could ever ask for, and your encouragement and support mean everything to me.

Thank you to Angela Charles for being with me every step of the way and keeping me organized.

Thank you to Renee Schultz for making the book so much better with your amazing graphics. Your talent is so inspiring, and I love the cover you designed for me.

Thank you to my sales buddies who allowed me to use their stories in this book: Michael Pyle, Bob Mesalam, Josh Cohen, and Grant Norris.

To the amazing team at Streamline Books, thank you! I would never have taken on this challenge if you hadn't found me and encouraged me to forge ahead. RuthAnne, you've been so lovely to work with, and your editing skills truly transformed my book.

Thank you to Diana Gelston and Robert Wittwer for being there with me from the beginning, encouraging me, and taking a chance on me. I'm forever grateful.

ABOUT THE AUTHOR

Katie Mullen is the founder of MMS Consulting, which delivers sales training and consulting to Fortune 500 companies. Prior to starting her business, Katie worked as a sales rep and was truly "in the trenches." After almost fifteen years in sales roles, Katie decided to pursue her passion of teaching the art and science of sales to others.

She is the host of the Golden Rule of Selling podcast and a regular contributor to LinkedIn. Her posts and podcasts reach millions of people each year. She has equipped thousands of sales reps around the country with her unique methods and tactics, using her customer research as the backbone of all the training.

Katie teaches sales reps how to sell in a way that makes

customers comfortable, because she keeps the focus *on them*. She teaches good sales reps how to be *great* sales reps.

Katie graduated Summa Cum Laude from the University of Kansas and lives in Kansas City with her husband, two kids, and a plethora of pets.

NOTES

1. Customer Insights: Research from Real Customers

1. Akavickaitė, Austėja. "Therapist Tries to Open Parents' Eyes by Sharing What 28 Teenagers and Kids Have Told Her." Bored Panda, October 21, 2022. https://www.boredpanda.com/family-trauma-counselor-shares-heartbreaking-things-kids-teens-said/?utm_source=google&utm_medium=organic&utm_campaign=organic.

2. Stop Annoying Customers: Understand Their Personality Profile

1. Merrill, David W., and Roger H. Reid. *Personal styles and effective performance: Make your style work.* Boca Raton: CRC Press, 1999.
2. Phillips, Bob. *The Delicate Art of Dancing with Porcupines: Learning to Appreciate the Finer Points of Others.* Ventura, CA: Regal Books, 1989.

3. The Science Behind Writing a Killer Email

1. "Email Etiquette for the Modern Professional." Boomerang for Gmail. Accessed August 23, 2023. https://www.boomeranggmail.com/l/email-etiquette.html.
2. "33 Tips for Optimizing B2B Sales Emails: The Ultimate Guide." SalesLoft. Accessed August 23, 2023. https://pages.salesloft.com/rs/432-WAJ-793/images/33%20Tips%20for%20Optimizing%20B2B%20Sales%20Emails%20eBook.pdf.
3. Stieglitz, Shira. "Your Typo Is Costing You 12% Extra on Your Google Ads Spend." Website Planet, August 22, 2023. https://www.websiteplanet.com/blog/grammar-report/.
4. "33 Tips for Optimizing B2B Sales Emails: The Ultimate Guide." SalesLoft.
5. "33 Tips for Optimizing B2B Sales Emails: The Ultimate Guide." SalesLoft.

4. The Art of Finding Customers

1. "Best Practices for Lead Response Management - MIT Study." CINC, May 20, 2021. https://help.cincpro.com/s/article/Best-Practices-for-Lead-Response-Management-MIT-Study.

5. Tackling the First 10 Seconds of the Prospecting Call

1. 30 Minutes to President's Club Podcast. https://www.30mpc.com/.
2. Sharma, Sakshi. "The Best Day & Time To Make Sales Calls In 2023." CallHippo, January 2, 2023. https://callhippo.com/blog/marketing/best-day-time-make-business-call.
3. "33 Tips for Optimizing B2B Sales Emails: The Ultimate Guide." SalesLoft.
4. "33 Tips for Optimizing B2B Sales Emails: The Ultimate Guide." SalesLoft.

6. Uncovering Pain Points Using the Magic Wedge Question

1. "Episode 04: Interview with a Customer: Meet Chris Nowak, Healthcare Technology Buyer – Part 2." MMS Consulting, November 2, 2020. https://www.mms-consulting.com/podcasts/episode4-eezag-y2ek3.

7. The Secret to Great Meetings and Presentations

1. Godfrey, Téa Silvestre. "10 Best Books for Learning the Art of Business Storytelling." Story Bistro, July 19, 2023. http://storybistro.com/best-books-learn-art-business-storytelling/.
2. Stevenson, Doug. How to Craft a Compelling Story with The Nine Steps of Story Structure, May 15, 2017. https://www.storytelling-in-business.com/nine-steps-of-story-structure/.

Notes

8. Social Selling: Why LinkedIn is Your Next Best Friend

1. "Fishing in the New Testament: A Misunderstood Analogy for Evangelism." Bible.org. Accessed August 23, 2023. https://bible.org/article/fishing-new-testament-misunderstood-analogy-evangelism.
2. Osman, Maddy. "Mind-Blowing LinkedIn Statistics and Facts (2023)." Kinsta®, March 21, 2023. https://kinsta.com/blog/linkedin-statistics/.

Made in the USA
Monee, IL
05 January 2025

73293561R00111